Reading STREET
Grade 1

Pearson Scott Foresman

Leveled Reader
Teaching Guide

D1305500

PEARSON

Glenview, Illinois • Boston, Massachusetts • Chandler, Arizona • Upper Saddle River, New Jersey

Accelerated Reader®

ISBN: 13: 978-0-328-48452-2
ISBN: 10:   0-328-48452-0
3 4 5 6 7 8 9 10 V031 13 12 11 10

Table of Contents

LEVELED READER TITLE	Instruction	Comprehension Practice	Vocabulary Practice
Carlos Picks a Pet	12–13	14	15
That Cat Needs Help!	16–17	18	19
Loni's Town	20–21	22	23
Baby Animals in the Rain Forest	24–25	26	27
Cary and the Wildlife Shelter	28–29	30	31
Around the World	32–33	34	35
Rules at School	36–37	38	39
School: Then and Now	40–41	42	43
Mom the Mayor	44–45	46	47
The Dinosaur Detectives	48–49	50	51
All About Food Chains	52–53	54	55
Bees and Beekeepers	56–57	58	59
A New Library	60–61	62	63
Paul's Bed	64–65	66	67
Britton Finds a Kitten	68–69	70	71
All About the Weather	72–73	74	75
Learn About Butterflies	76–77	78	79
Monarchs Migrate South	80–81	82	83

Graphic Organizers

Introduction

Scott Foresman *Reading Street* provides more than 750 leveled readers that help children become better readers and build a lifelong love of reading. The *Reading Street* leveled readers are engaging texts that help children practice critical reading skills and strategies. They also provide opportunities to build vocabulary, understand concepts, and develop reading fluency.

The leveled readers were developed to be age-appropriate and appealing to children at each grade level. The leveled readers consist of engaging texts in a variety of genres, including fantasy, folk tales, realistic fiction, historical fiction, and narrative and expository nonfiction. To better address real-life reading skills that children will encounter in testing situations and beyond, a higher percentage of nonfiction texts is provided at each grade.

USING THE LEVELED READERS

You can use the leveled readers to meet the diverse needs of your children. Consider using the readers to

- practice critical skills and strategies
- build fluency
- build vocabulary and concepts
- build background for the main selections in the student book
- provide a variety of reading experiences, e.g., shared, group, individual, take-home, readers' theater

GUIDED READING APPROACH

The *Reading Street* leveled readers are leveled according to Guided Reading criteria by experts trained in Guided Reading. The Guided Reading levels increase in difficulty within a grade level and across grade levels. In addition to leveling according to Guided Reading criteria, the instruction provided in the *Leveled Reader Teaching Guide* is compatible with Guided Reading instruction. An instructional routine is provided for each leveled reader. This routine is most effective when working with individual children or small groups.

MANAGING THE CLASSROOM

When using the leveled readers with individuals or small groups, you'll want to keep the other children engaged in meaningful, independent learning tasks. Establishing independent practice stations throughout the classroom and child routines for these stations can help you manage the rest of the class while you work with individuals or small groups. Practice stations can include listening, phonics, vocabulary, independent reading, and cross-curricular activities. For classroom management, create a work board that lists the stations and which children should be at each station. Provide instructions at each station that detail the tasks to be accomplished. Update the board and alert children when they should rotate to a new station. For additional support for managing your classroom, see the *Reading Street* Practice Stations' *Classroom Management Handbook.*

USING THE LEVELED READER TEACHING GUIDE

The *Leveled Reader Teaching Guide* provides an instruction plan for each leveled reader based on the same instructional routine.

INTRODUCE THE BOOK The Introduction includes suggestions for creating interest in the text by discussing the title and author, building background, and previewing the book and its features.

READ THE BOOK Before children begin reading the book, have them set purposes for reading and discuss how they can use the reading strategy as they read. Determine how you want children in a particular group to read the text—softly or silently, to a specific point, or the entire text. Then use the Comprehension Questions to provide support as needed and to assess comprehension.

REVISIT THE BOOK The Think and Share questions provide opportunities for children to demonstrate their understanding of the text, the target comprehension skill, and vocabulary. The Response Options require children to revisit the text to respond to what they've read and to move beyond the text to explore related content.

SKILL WORK The Skill Work box provides instruction and practice for the target skill and strategy and selection vocabulary. Instruction for an alternate comprehension skill allows teachers to provide additional skill instruction and practice for children.

USING THE GRAPHIC ORGANIZERS

Graphic organizers in blackline-master format can be found on pages 132–153. These can be used as overhead transparencies or as worksheets.

ASSESSING PERFORMANCE

Use the assessment forms that begin on page 6 to make notes about your children's reading skills, use of reading strategies, and general reading behaviors.

MEASURE FLUENT READING (pp. 6–7) Provides directions for measuring a child's fluency, based on words correct per minute (wcpm), and reading accuracy using a running record.

OBSERVATION CHECKLIST (p. 8) Allows you to note the regularity with which children demonstrate their understanding and use of reading skills and strategies.

READING BEHAVIORS CHECKLIST (p. 9) Provides criteria for monitoring certain reading behaviors.

READING STRATEGY ASSESSMENT (p. 10) Provides criteria for evaluating each child's proficiency as a strategic reader.

PROGRESS REPORT (p. 11) Provides a means to track a child's book-reading progress over a period of time by noting the level at which a child reads and his or her accuracy at that level. Reading the chart from left to right gives you a visual model of how quickly a child is making the transition from one level to the next. Share these reports with parents or guardians to help them see how their child's reading is progressing.

Measure
Fluent Reading

Taking a Running Record

A running record is an assessment of a child's oral reading accuracy and oral reading fluency. Reading accuracy is based on the number of words read correctly. Reading fluency is based on the reading rate (the number of words correct per minute) and the degree to which a child reads with a "natural flow."

How to Measure Reading Accuracy

1. Choose a grade-level text of about 80 to 120 words that is unfamiliar to the child.
2. Make a copy of the text for yourself. Make a copy for the child or have the child read aloud from a book.
3. Give the child the text and have the child read aloud. (You may wish to record the child's reading for later evaluation.)
4. On your copy of the text, mark any miscues or errors the child makes while reading. See the running record sample on page 7, which shows how to identify and mark miscues.
5. Count the total number of words in the text and the total number of errors made by the child. Note: If a child makes the same error more than once, such as mispronouncing the same word multiple times, count it as one error. Self-corrections do not count as actual errors. Use the following formula to calculate the percentage score, or accuracy rate:

$$\frac{\text{Total Number of Words} - \text{Total Number of Errors}}{\text{Total Number of Words}} \times 100 = \text{percentage score}$$

Interpreting the Results

- A child who reads **95–100%** of the words correctly is reading at an **independent level** and may need more challenging text.
- A child who reads **90–94%** of the words correctly is reading at an **instructional level** and will likely benefit from guided instruction.
- A child who reads **89%** or fewer of the words correctly is reading at a **frustrational level** and may benefit most from targeted instruction with lower-level texts and intervention.

How to Measure Reading Rate (WCPM)

1. Follow Steps 1–3 above.
2. Note the exact times when the child begins and finishes reading.
3. Use the following formula to calculate the number of words correct per minute (WCPM):

$$\frac{\text{Total Number of Words Read Correctly}}{\text{Total Number of Seconds}} \times 60 = \text{words correct per minute}$$

Interpreting the Results

By the end of the year, a first-grader should be reading approximately 45–60 WCPM.

Running Record Sample

Running Record Sample

Beth and her friends were eating — 6
(lunch) in the park. — 10

"Tell us about your trip to the — 17
beach," Beth said to one of her friends. — 25

"It was great! /grēt/" her friend said. — 31

Beth's friends talked about sports, — 36
and they talked about movies. But Beth — 43
was not talking. ^and She was looking away. — 50

"Beth?" they called to her. — 55

Beth did not speak. She was looking — 62
at bird. It had landed on a sign. Beth — 71
just stared. (sc) — 73

"I have a feeling," Beth said at last. — 81

"What does that mean?" her friends — 87
asked. — 88

Beth took out her drawing pad. "I — 95
(H)
need to draw that bird, " ~~she~~ Beth said. — 102

Notations

Accurate Reading
The child reads a word correctly.

Omission
The child omits words or word parts.

Mispronunciation/Misreading
The child pronounces or reads a word incorrectly.

Insertion
The child inserts words or parts of words that are not in the text.

Self-correction
The child reads a word incorrectly but then corrects the error. Do not count self-corrections as actual errors. However, noting self-corrections will help you identify words the child finds difficult.

Hesitation
The child hesitates over a word, and the teacher provides the word. Wait several seconds before telling the child what the word is.

Substitution
The child substitutes words or parts of words for the words in the text.

Running Record Results

Total Number of Words: **102**

Number of Errors: **5**

Reading Time: **136 seconds**

▶ **Reading Accuracy**

$$\frac{102 - 5}{102} \times 100 = 95.098 = 95\%$$

Accuracy Percentage Score: **95%**

▶ **Reading Rate—WCPM**

$$\frac{97}{136} \times 60 = 42.794 = 43 \text{ words correct per minute}$$

Reading Rate: **43 WCPM**

Observation Checklist

Child's Name _____ Date _____

Behaviors Observed	Always (Proficient)	Usually (Fluent)	Sometimes (Developing)	Rarely (Novice)

Reading Strategies and Skills

Behaviors Observed	Always (Proficient)	Usually (Fluent)	Sometimes (Developing)	Rarely (Novice)
Uses prior knowledge and preview to understand what book is about				
Makes predictions and checks them while reading				
Uses context clues to figure out meanings of new words				
Uses phonics and syllabication to decode words				
Self-corrects while reading				
Reads at an appropriate reading rate				
Reads with appropriate intonation and stress				
Uses fix-up strategies				
Identifies story elements: character, setting, plot, theme				
Summarizes plot or main ideas accurately				
Uses target comprehension skill to understand the text better				
Responds thoughtfully about the text				

Reading Behaviors and Attitudes

Behaviors Observed	Always (Proficient)	Usually (Fluent)	Sometimes (Developing)	Rarely (Novice)
Enjoys listening to stories				
Chooses reading as a free-time activity				
Reads with sustained interest and attention				
Participates in discussion about books				

General Comments

Reading Behaviors Checklist

Child's Name _____   Date _____

Behavior	Yes	No	Not Applicable
Recognizes letters of the alphabet			
Recognizes name in print			
Recognizes some environmental print, such as signs and logos			
Knows the difference between letters and words			
Knows the difference between capital and lowercase letters			
Understands function of capitalization and punctuation			
Recognizes that book parts, such as the cover, title page, and table of contents, offer information			
Recognizes that words are represented in writing by specific sequences of letters			
Recognizes words that rhyme			
Distinguishes rhyming and nonrhyming words			
Knows letter-sound correspondences			
Identifies and isolates initial sounds in words			
Identifies and isolates final sounds in words			
Blends sounds to make spoken words			
Segments one-syllable spoken words into individual phonemes			
Reads consonant blends and digraphs			
Reads and understands endings, such as *-es, -ed, -ing*			
Reads vowels and vowel diphthongs			
Reads and understands possessives			
Reads and understands compound words			
Reads simple sentences			
Reads simple stories			
Understands simple story structure			
Other:			

Reading Strategy Assessment ✓

Child _____ Date _____

Teacher _____

		Proficient	Developing	Emerging	Not showing trait
Building Background Comments:	Previews	☐	☐	☐	☐
	Asks questions	☐	☐	☐	☐
	Predicts	☐	☐	☐	☐
	Activates prior knowledge	☐	☐	☐	☐
	Sets own purposes for reading	☐	☐	☐	☐
	Other:	☐	☐	☐	☐
Comprehension Comments:	Retells/summarizes	☐	☐	☐	☐
	Questions, evaluates ideas	☐	☐	☐	☐
	Relates to self/other texts	☐	☐	☐	☐
	Paraphrases	☐	☐	☐	☐
	Rereads/reads ahead for meaning	☐	☐	☐	☐
	Visualizes	☐	☐	☐	☐
	Uses decoding strategies	☐	☐	☐	☐
	Uses vocabulary strategies	☐	☐	☐	☐
	Understands key ideas of a text	☐	☐	☐	☐
	Other:	☐	☐	☐	☐
Fluency Comments:	Adjusts reading rate	☐	☐	☐	☐
	Reads for accuracy	☐	☐	☐	☐
	Uses expression	☐	☐	☐	☐
	Other:	☐	☐	☐	☐
Connections Comments:	Relates text to self	☐	☐	☐	☐
	Relates text to text	☐	☐	☐	☐
	Relates text to world	☐	☐	☐	☐
	Other:	☐	☐	☐	☐
Self-Assessment Comments:	Is aware of: Strengths	☐	☐	☐	☐
	Needs	☐	☐	☐	☐
	Improvement/achievement	☐	☐	☐	☐
	Sets and implements learning goals	☐	☐	☐	☐
	Maintains logs, records, portfolio	☐	☐	☐	☐
	Works with others	☐	☐	☐	☐
	Shares ideas and materials	☐	☐	☐	☐
	Other:	☐	☐	☐	☐

Progress Report

Child's Name _____

At the top of the chart, record the book title, its grade/unit/week (for example, 1.2.3), and the child's accuracy percentage. See page 6 for measuring fluency, calculating accuracy and reading rates. At the bottom of the chart, record the date you took the running record. In the middle of the chart, make an X in the box across from the level of the child's reading—frustrational level (below 89% accuracy), instructional level (90–94% accuracy), or independent level (95–100% accuracy). Record the reading rate (WCPM) in the next row.

Book Title					
Grade/Unit/Week					
Reading Accuracy Percentage					
LEVEL — **Frustrational** (89% or below)					
LEVEL — **Instructional** (90–94%)					
LEVEL — **Independent** (95% or above)					
Reading Rate (WCPM)					
Date					

Carlos Picks a Pet

SUMMARY Carlos visits an animal shelter in search of a pet. He learns about various animals and their needs before choosing a pet cat.

LESSON VOCABULARY

needs   responsibility
shelter

INTRODUCE THE BOOK

INTRODUCE THE TITLE AND AUTHOR Discuss with children the title and author of *Carlos Picks a Pet*. Based on the title, ask children to predict who Carlos might be and what might happen in this book.

BUILD BACKGROUND Invite children to talk about their experiences with pets. Ask: What animals make good pets? What animals don't make good pets? Also, discuss the various ways in which people can find pets to adopt.

ELL Ask English language learners to share pet-related vocabulary from their home language.

PREVIEW/TAKE A PICTURE WALK Have children look through the book and examine the photographs. Focus their attention on the thought bubble on page 5. Discuss this device and how it tells the reader what the character is thinking. Together, generate a few questions about the story and list the questions on chart paper. Later, review the questions as a group and see how many the class can answer.

READ THE BOOK

SET PURPOSE Have children set a purpose for reading *Carlos Picks a Pet*. Suggest they focus on one or two things they would like to learn about pets. As they read, have them look for information that relates to these topics.

STRATEGY SUPPORT: MONITOR AND FIX UP If, during class discussion, children do not recall specific details about the story, model how to reread the text for forgotten information. For example: "Why didn't Carlos choose a dog? I forget. Let's read that part again to see. Oh yes, he lives in the city and would have to walk a dog. I didn't notice that the first time."

COMPREHENSION QUESTIONS

PAGE 3 How does Carlos find out about pets and their needs? How else could he have learned? (*Possible responses: Carlos learns about pets by visiting an animal shelter; he could have read a book or talked to somebody who has a pet.*)

PAGE 7 What is one responsibility a dog owner has? (*Possible response: Dog owners need to walk their dogs at least twice a day.*)

PAGE 10 Would you want Carlos to take care of your pet? Why or why not? (*Possible response: Yes, because he knows what pets need to stay safe and healthy.*)

PAGE 11 Which of the pets in this book would you choose? Why? (*Responses will vary, but should relate to some of the considerations mentioned in the story.*)

REVISIT THE BOOK

THINK AND SHARE

1. Responses will vary.
2. He thinks a rabbit might chew on things that could hurt it.
3. Possible responses: He learns about each animal's *needs.* Then he thinks about the *responsibility* of owning different kinds of pets.
4. Responses will vary.

EXTEND UNDERSTANDING Ask children to compare the thought bubbles on pages 5, 7, and 9. Ask: What is different about the thought bubble on page 9? What do the stars tell you?

RESPONSE OPTIONS

WRITING Invite children to write a poem about a pet they own or a pet they would like to own. Ask them to think of words or phrases that remind them of the pet. Then have them use these words in their poem.

SCIENCE CONNECTION

Suggest that children choose one pet from the story and make a poster to inform others about its needs and care. They can learn more about the pet from books, brochures, or the Internet.

TIME FOR **Science**

Skill Work

TEACH/REVIEW VOCABULARY

Turn to page 3. Read the sentence containing the word *responsibility.* Invite children to figure out what responsibility means, based on the sentence and what they already know. Ask: Is cleaning your room a responsibility? Is watching TV? Repeat for *needs* (page 3) and *shelter* (page 4).

TARGET SKILL AND STRATEGY

CHARACTER Point out to children that Carlos is a character. Discuss Carlos's actions and what they reveal about his thoughts and feelings. Ask: When Carlos promises to bring his cat to the vet, what does this tell you about him?

MONITOR AND FIX UP Children sometimes think that they should be able to answer questions about a story after a single reading. Let them know that it is okay—and often a good idea—to read a passage more than once and to continue to ask themselves comprehension questions.

ADDITIONAL SKILL INSTRUCTION

COMPARE AND CONTRAST Point out to children that when they read, they can think about how two things are alike and how they are different. Guide children in comparing rabbits and cats. Make a T-chart with two column headings: *Rabbits* and *Cats.* Turn to page 4. Have children review the text and identify the characteristics of rabbits. List these in the appropriate column on the chart. Turn to page 8 and review and list cats' characteristics. Then read the chart together. Identify and circle the characteristics that both animals share.

Name _____

Character

1. Write what Carlos thinks about rabbits.

_____

_____

_____

2. Write what Carlos thinks about dogs.

_____

_____

_____

3. Write what Carlos thinks about cats.

_____

_____

_____

4. Draw Carlos and Spots. Show how Carlos feels at the end of the story.

Name _____

Vocabulary

Use a word from the box to complete the sentence.

Words to Know
needs   responsibility   shelter

1. Taking care of a pet is a big _____ .

2. Food and water are two of a pet's _____ .

3. Carlos found his pet at the animal _____ .

4. Write a sentence that tells about your needs.

_____

_____

_____

_____

5. Write a sentence that tells about a responsibility.

_____

_____

_____

_____

That Cat Needs Help!

SUMMARY When Mr. Green's cat gets stuck in a tree, a variety of community helpers pitch in to help.

LESSON VOCABULARY
career
service
tools

INTRODUCE THE BOOK

INTRODUCE THE TITLE AND AUTHOR Discuss with children the title and the author of *That Cat Needs Help!* Ask children what they think the book might be about, based on the title and the cover illustration.

BUILD BACKGROUND Ask children if they can think of a time when an animal needed help. If they cannot recall any examples from their own experience, ask them to recall books and movies. Who helped the animal? How? Tell children that they will be reading a book about an animal that needs help. As they read, they can think about how the story relates to what they already know.

PREVIEW As children look through the book, encourage them to generate questions about the story, based on the illustrations. Think aloud: I see that the dog is chasing the cat and the man is chasing the dog. I wonder what will happen next?

READ THE BOOK

SET PURPOSE Have children set a purpose for reading *That Cat Needs Help!* Recall the questions you and the children generated while looking at the illustrations. Suggest reading on to find answers to these questions. For instance, "I wonder what the police officer, firefighter, and vet will do in this story. I think I'll read and find out."

STRATEGY SUPPORT: SUMMARIZE As children summarize the book, have them think about how they would tell the story to a friend who hasn't read it yet. Suggest that they take notes as they read, using words and pictures to help them remember the important parts of the story.

COMPREHENSION QUESTIONS

PAGE 3 Why is the cat running away? Why is Mr. Green chasing the dog and the cat? *(Possible answer: The cat is running from the dog. Mr. Green wants to make sure the cat doesn't get hurt.)*

PAGE 5 How did the cat get into the tree? *(The cat probably climbed into the tree.)*

PAGES 6–9 If you were the little girl in this story and needed to ask someone for help, who would you choose? Why? *(Possible answer: The police officer, because police officers help people who are in trouble.)*

PAGES 8–9 What tool does the firefighter use? How does it help him? Could this really happen? *(He uses a ladder to climb into the tree. Yes, firefighters do use ladders.)*

PAGE 11 What do you think happened after the cat went to the vet? *(Responses will vary, but should relate to the story's characters and events.)*

REVISIT THE BOOK

THINK AND SHARE

1. Possible response: Beginning: A cat gets stuck in a tree. Middle: A girl gets help. End: A firefighter gets the cat down from the tree.
2. Possible response: The little girl asked Officer Kim for help. Officer Kim called the fire department. The firefighter got the cat down.
3. *Kix*
4. Possible answer: I would have held the dog while the vet checked the cat.

EXTEND UNDERSTANDING Guide children to notice the setting of the story. Ask: Does the story take place in the city or the country? What time of year is it? How can you tell?

RESPONSE OPTIONS

WRITING Challenge children to think of another way to get the cat out of the tree. Have them write a sentence or two, and invite them to illustrate the sentence.

SOCIAL STUDIES CONNECTION

Talk with children about what to do in case of an emergency. Discuss situations in which it is necessary to call for help. Make sure that children know their local emergency telephone number.

Skill Work

TEACH/REVIEW VOCABULARY

To reinforce children's understanding of words in context, read the sentence on page 6 that contains the word *service*. Ask: What does *service* mean? Can you think of another word for *service*? Continue for *tools* (page 8) and *career* (page 10).

ELL Make sure that English language learners understand the names and roles of the community helpers mentioned in the story: *police, firefighter,* and *vet.* Use word cards and illustrations to introduce each word. Then divide children into groups and assign each group a word card to act out. Have the rest of the children guess the word.

TARGET SKILL AND STRATEGY

PLOT Remind children that every story has a beginning, middle, and end. Stories usually start with a problem and end with a solution. Remembering these parts of the story makes it easier for them to tell the story in their own words. As children read, suggest that they use a story map to record what happens first, next, and last. Ask them to find the problem and solution in the story.

SUMMARIZE Point out to children that putting a story in their own words can help them better understand a story. As children read, have them describe the main characters and tell what happens. Ask: What was the girl trying to do? Did things work out the way she wanted?

ADDITIONAL SKILL INSTRUCTION

COMPARE AND CONTRAST Explain to children that when they *compare* two things, they tell how they are the same. When they *contrast* two things, they tell how they are different. Ask children to tell how Officer Kim and the firefighter are alike and different.

Name _____

Plot

The **plot** is what happens in a story.
Answer the questions about *That Cat Needs Help!*

1. What is the problem in this story?

_____

- -

_____

_____

2. Who does the little girl ask for help?

_____

- -

_____

_____

3. Who is called next?

_____

- -

_____

_____

4. What is the solution to the problem?

_____

- -

_____

Name _____

Vocabulary

Circle the word that best completes each sentence.
Write it on the line.

1. Officer Kim has worked in our town since the beginning of her

   _____

   _____ .

   canoe   career   canine

2. The firefighter said, "I know what _____

   we need.

   tooth   tools   too

3. The veterinarian was happy to be of _____ .

   serpent   surprise   service

Loni's Town

SUMMARY Loni and her grandmother reflect on how their town has changed over the years.

LESSON VOCABULARY

past	present
transportation	produce

INTRODUCE THE BOOK

INTRODUCE THE TITLE AND AUTHOR Discuss with children the title and author of *Loni's Town*. Invite them to look closely at the cover illustration. Point out the girl and the woman looking out the window. Ask children to predict, based on the title, cover, and their prior experience, whether the book will be like real life or make-believe.

BUILD BACKGROUND Show children a picture that was taken long ago. Discuss the age of the picture and invite children to talk about other old pictures they have seen. If children have seen old family pictures, have them share their experiences.

ELL Invite children to talk about the place where they and their families came from. Have them discuss how it has changed over time.

PREVIEW/TAKE A PICTURE WALK Invite children to turn the pages and preview the illustrations. Turn to the title page. Think aloud: "It looks like this illustration shows something that happened a long time ago." Turn to page 3. Ask children to read the signs on the storefronts. Turn to pages 4 and 5. Have children compare the two illustrations. Ask: Is the picture on page 5 old or new? Have children tell what they think is happening on pages 6 and 7. Turn to page 9. Ask: Where have we seen this building before? Turn to pages 10 and 11 and invite children to predict how the story might end.

READ THE BOOK

SET PURPOSE Have children set a purpose for reading *Loni's Town*. Suggest that they review the illustrations and think about what they would like find out about the story.

STRATEGY SUPPORT: VISUALIZE Ask children to close their eyes and listen as you read page 6 aloud. Guide them as they visualize the barn. Suggest that they compare the barn to others they have seen. Then have children open their eyes and draw the scene as they imagined it.

COMPREHENSION QUESTIONS

PAGES 3–5 Do you think this story is taking place now, or in the past? What makes you think so? (*Responses will vary, but should include details from the text. Possible answer: The story is taking place now, but Loni's grandma is remembering things that happened in the past. She is showing Loni old pictures.*)

PAGE 4 How would you describe Loni's town? Is it like any place you have ever seen? (*Responses will vary according to children's personal experience.*)

PAGE 7 How do you think Loni's grandma learned about what happened in the past? (*Possible response: Somebody told her stories and gave her pictures.*)

PAGE 10 Compare the illustration on this page to the illustration on page 4. What is the same? What has changed? (*Possible response: The steeple in the background is the same. The road, buildings, and people have changed.*)

PAGE 11 How might Loni's town change in the future? Why do you think so? (*Responses will vary.*)

REVISIT THE BOOK

THINK AND SHARE

1. Responses will vary, but should relate to how Loni was portrayed in the book. Possible responses: good listener, friendly, curious, happy
2. Responses will vary, but could include descriptive details like "a field of corn stretched down to the river."
3. Possible response: It means that things are different.
4. Responses will vary.

EXTEND UNDERSTANDING Discuss how transportation changed over time in this story. Suggest that children create a time line that shows the ways people traveled when Loni's great-great-great grandmother was a girl, when Loni's great-grandmother was born, when Loni's grandmother was a girl, and today.

RESPONSE OPTIONS

WORD WORK Discuss the multiple meanings of the word *present*. Model how to look up the word's definition in a children's dictionary. Challenge children to make up a sentence for each meaning of present. Repeat for the word *change*.

SOCIAL STUDIES CONNECTION

Time For SOCIAL STUDIES

Encourage children to find out what their community looked like 100 years ago. Offer assistance as they conduct research on the Internet or in the school library. Suggest that they work together to create a visual display comparing their town in the past and present.

Skill Work

TEACH/REVIEW VOCABULARY

Turn to page 5 and read the sentence that contains the word *past*. Ask children what it means if something is in the past. Encourage children to make up a new sentence using the word. Repeat for *produce* (page 7), *transportation* (page 9), and *present* (page 11). Then introduce children to the word *synonym*. Explain that a synonym is a word that has the same (or almost the same) meaning as another word. Ask children to think of a synonym for each word. Compile a class list of synonyms.

TARGET SKILL AND STRATEGY

CHARACTER AND SETTING Point out to children that *characters* are the people or animals in stories. Characters can be real or they can be made up. When good readers read a story, they think about what the characters say and do. They also think about when and where the story happens. As children read *Loni's Town*, invite them to discuss the characters and setting. Ask: How does Loni feel about her grandma? What does Loni's grandma think about her town? Have children describe the setting of each scene and support their ideas with details.

VISUALIZE Point out to children that when they read a story, they can picture it in their minds. *Visualizing* a story can give readers a better understanding of the characters and setting of *Loni's Town*. Invite children read, model how to visualize the setting and characters. Think aloud: I am walking down the street past a bakery. I see wonderful cakes and cookies in the window. I smell bread baking.

ADDITIONAL SKILL INSTRUCTION

THEME Remind children that thinking about what they know from their lives can help readers understand the "big idea" of a story. Invite children to discuss the "big idea" of *Loni's Town*. Ask: What did Loni learn in this story? How does that relate to your life?

Name _____

Character and Setting

Think about the **characters** in the story. Think about the **setting** or where and when the story happened. Then answer the questions below.

1. What does Grandma think about the town?

_____

- -

_____

2. How does Grandma feel when she shows pictures to Loni?

_____

- -

_____

3. How does Grandma feel at the end of the story?

_____

- -

_____

4. What is Loni's town like today?

_____

- -

_____

5. When does the story take place?

_____

- -

_____

Name _____

Vocabulary

Choose a word from the box to complete each sentence.

Words to Know

present   past   transportation   produce

1. In the _____, Loni's family lives in an apartment building.

2. In the _____, Loni's relatives lived on farms.

3. Years ago, people used horses and boats for _____ _____ .

4. They kept chickens to _____ eggs.

5. Write a sentence that tells where you live in the present.

_____

_____

_____

Baby Animals in the Rain Forest

SUMMARY Baby tapirs, sloths, parrots, marmosets, and butterflies are the rain forest animals described in this informational nonfiction book.

LESSON VOCABULARY

observe   parent
wild

INTRODUCE THE BOOK

INTRODUCE THE TITLE AND AUTHOR Point out the title and the author of *Baby Animals in the Rain Forest* to children. Based on the title and the cover, ask children if they think this book will be about animals that live in nature or animals that live with people. Remind them to give reasons for their predictions.

BUILD BACKGROUND Play a recording of rain forest sounds for the children. (Many such recordings are available for download from the Internet.) Ask children to listen for different kinds of animals. Tell children that the animals they hear live in a rain forest. If they do not know what a rain forest is, ask them what they think it might be, based on its name. Then brainstorm ways of finding the definition of the term. Model how to look up *rain forest* in a children's encyclopedia or other reference work.

PREVIEW/TAKE A PICTURE WALK As children look through the book and examine the illustrations and captions, model how to generate "I wonder" statements and questions about what they see: "I wonder what this striped animal is on the cover. It looks sort of like an elephant. What is it called? I want to read and find out more."

READ THE BOOK

SET PURPOSE Have children set a purpose for reading *Baby Animals in the Rain Forest*. Remind children of the questions they generated while previewing the book. Suggest that the children think about what they want to learn as they read.

STRATEGY SUPPORT: IMPORTANT IDEAS Explain to children that some ideas in a story are more important than others. Good readers look for important ideas as they read. Important ideas tell more about the main idea. Model finding an important idea on page 5: I read that baby tapirs have stripes and spots. The caption says that these stripes and spots help a baby tapir hide. These both tell more about baby animals, so these are important ideas.

COMPREHENSION QUESTIONS

PAGE 5 Think of a question to ask about tapirs. *(Responses will vary.)*

PAGE 6 What are these sentences all about? *(The passage is about birds.)*

PAGES 7–8 How are sloths like monkeys? How are they different? *(Possible response: Both hang in trees, and the babies and parents look alike. Monkeys are fast and sloths are slow.)*

PAGE 9 Are the animals in this illustration babies or adults? How can you tell? *(babies; responses will vary, but should relate to what children have learned elsewhere in the text.)*

REVISIT THE BOOK

THINK AND SHARE

1. Page 8 is about a baby sloth and its mom.
2. Possible response: I learned that baby animals don't always look like their parents. This helped me understand why they looked different in the pictures.
3. A wild animal is born and lives in nature.
4. The picture should show a caterpillar and a butterfly.

EXTEND UNDERSTANDING Invite children to discuss the illustrations. Ask: Do the illustrations help you understand what the plants and animals of the rain forest look like? What did you learn from the illustrations? Which is your favorite illustration? Why?

RESPONSE OPTIONS

WRITING Suggest that children imagine that they are visiting the rain forest. Ask them to write a few sentences about what they can see, hear, and smell.

SCIENCE CONNECTION

TIME FOR
Science

Children can choose one animal from the book to research independently. Provide an assortment of resources for children to explore, including nature magazines and other photographic guides. Suggest that children try and identify the bird or butterfly species pictured in *Baby Animals of the Rain Forest.*

Skill Work

TEACH/REVIEW VOCABULARY

Write the word *wild* on the board. Turn to page 3. Ask children if they can find this word on the page. Read the sentence together. Then ask children if they can think of another word that means wild. List the children's suggestions on the board. Make a T-chart that lists the author's words in the left-hand column and the children's synonyms in the right-hand column. Continue for the other vocabulary words.

ELL Make sure that the children know the names of the animals in the book. Review the illustrations on each page and have children label the illustrations with sticky notes. Encourage children to share corresponding words from their home languages.

TARGET SKILL AND STRATEGY

MAIN IDEA Turn to page 5. Read the passage together. Ask: What are these sentences all about? Are the sentences about plants? Are they about food? Guide children to see that the sentences are about tapirs.

IMPORTANT IDEAS Remind children that *important ideas* are the little pieces of information that support the main ideas, and that some ideas are more important than others. Ask: What is an important idea that you read? What is an idea that you read that is interesting, but maybe not as important?

ADDITIONAL SKILL INSTRUCTION

AUTHOR'S PURPOSE Remind children that someone wrote this book. Melissa Burke, the author, decided what information to include and how to write it. Point out that the author included information about whether baby animals and their parents look alike. Ask: Why do you think she did this?

Name _____

Main Idea

Read the passage. Then answer the questions.

Here are some twin baby monkeys. Older monkeys watch the younger ones. They give them rides on their backs in the trees. They feed them and play with them. They teach them lots of things.

I. What is this paragraph all about?

_____
- -
_____
- -
_____

2. Write two facts you learned about baby monkeys.

_____
- -
_____
- -
_____
- -
_____

Draw an older monkey playing with a baby monkey.

Name _____

Vocabulary

Draw a line from the word to its definition.

1. observe   mother or father

2. wild   watch

3. parent   born and living in nature

4. Write a sentence using the words **wild** and **parent**.

_____

- -

_____

- -

_____

- -

_____

Cary and the Wildlife Shelter

SUMMARY This fictional story is about Cary and her mom's visit to a shelter for wild animals that live nearby. They help plant a garden filled with flowers and plants for the animals to eat. Cary and her mom return later to see the animals enjoying the new "wildlife buffet."

LESSON VOCABULARY

habitat   hatch

survive

INTRODUCE THE BOOK

INTRODUCE THE TITLE AND AUTHOR Discuss with children the title and the author of *Cary and the Wildlife Shelter*. Invite the children to describe what they see happening on the cover. Have them say the names of the different plants and animals they know. Also encourage children to describe how they think the title relates to the illustration. Ask: What does the word "wildlife" mean? What wildlife do you see on the cover? What does "shelter" mean? How does that relate to all of the animals that are eating in the picture? What do you think this girl has to do with the animals and their food?

BUILD BACKGROUND Engage children in a discussion of wildlife and other animals. Ask what they know about different animals, where they live, and what they eat. Also encourage children to share their experiences with wild animals, including trips to the zoo, aquarium, shelters, or other places they may have seen or learned about wild animals.

PREVIEW Have children preview the book by looking at each illustration. Encourage children to describe what they see happening in the pictures and predict what they think the story might be about. Ask: What do you think the girl and her mom are learning about these animals? Why do you think these other people are there? What do you think they are going to do?

READ THE BOOK

SET PURPOSE Encourage children to set a purpose for reading the book. Based on your discussion of the title and cover illustration, ask children what they would like to find out about this story. Ask: What do you think we will learn about these animals in this story? Are you interested in finding out what this girl has to do with the animals? What other illustrations in the book are you curious about? Why?

STRATEGY SUPPORT: STORY STRUCTURE Tell children that stories are arranged in an order from beginning to end. Each event in the story leads to the next event. When they think about how all these events fit together, they can tell what the story is all about.

COMPREHENSION QUESTIONS

PAGE 4 Why was Cary so excited when they got to the shelter? *(because she loved animals and now she was getting a chance to do something to help them)*

PAGE 7 Bev explains that animals can't survive without what two things? *(a habitat, or a place to live, and food to eat)*

PAGE 9 Why are they only going to use plants that grow naturally in a special buffet? *(so the animals do not get used to any foods they would not find in their natural habitat)*

PAGE 10 Why do you think the volunteers felt proud of their work? *(because they worked hard and did something to help the animals)*

PAGE 11 Why was the wildlife buffet a big success? *(Many different animals came to eat and enjoy the wildlife buffet.)*

REVISIT THE BOOK

THINK AND SHARE

1. Possible response: that wild animals live in our neighborhood and may need help, even from children
2. Possible response: Beginning: Cary and her mom go to the WIldlife Shelter. Middle: Cary and the group work on a project to plant food for animals. End: Cary and her mom go back to see that their project was a big success.
3. Responses will vary but the vowel sound of the words on children's pages must include a short *e*.
4. Responses will vary. Make sure children provide reasons for their answers.

EXTEND UNDERSTANDING Turn to page 8, and call children's attention to the poster Bev is using to explain their plans for the wildlife buffet. Have children read the words and describe the pictures on the poster. Ask: How does this poster help show Cary and the other volunteers what they are going to be doing? How does this poster help you understand the story and the meaning of a "wildlife buffet"?

RESPONSE OPTIONS

WRITING Ask children to imagine what they would do on a trip to a wildlife shelter. Have them write a couple of short sentences about the plants and animals they might see there.

SCIENCE CONNECTION

Help children research the foods that common wildlife in your area, such as birds, squirrels, or chipmunks, like to eat. Work together to plant or gather these foods to create your own "wildlife buffet" for the animals. Also, talk about the importance of helping preserve wildlife, and creating as natural a habitat as possible for them. If possible, take a field trip to the zoo or invite a wildlife expert to come speak to the class about animals and habitats.

Skill Work

TEACH/REVIEW VOCABULARY
Write out the vocabulary words and model for children how to sound out and pronounce each word. Help children determine the meanings of the words by using each in a sentence, for example, "Baby chicks *hatch* from their eggs." Do the same for each word. As children come up with definitions for each word, write them down for children to refer to as they read.

TARGET SKILL AND STRATEGY

MAIN IDEA Remind children that the *main idea* is what a story or book is mostly about. Ask children what this book is about *(a shelter for wild animals)*. After reading *Cary and the Wildlife Shelter*, ask children to state things that all wild animals need. Introduce the idea that natural habitats are being lost and that people, even children, can help animals to survive.

STORY STRUCTURE As children read, have them keep track of what happens in the beginning, middle, and end of the story. Keeping track of what happens in the story will help them learn more about the characters and what happens to them.

ADDITIONAL SKILL INSTRUCTION

SEQUENCE As children follow the events and structure of the story from beginning to middle to end, guide them in understanding that each event leads to another. It may be helpful to use signal words such as *first, next, then,* and *last.* Ask: When Cary and her mom go to the wildlife shelter, what do they do? After they plant the garden, what happens? What do they see when they go back?

Name _____

Main Idea

Read the passage. Then answer the questions.

Long ago, wild animals lived far from people. Now some wild animals are losing their homes. Why? Because people are moving into the animals' natural habitats. People are building houses where the wild animals once lived.

1. What is the main idea of this paragraph?

_____

_____

_____

_____

2. Write two details that tell you about the main idea.

_____

_____

_____

3. Draw two wild animals that live in your neighborhood.

Name _____

Vocabulary

Draw a line to match each word to its meaning.

1. habitat   a. to live

2. hatch   b. a place where plants and
                                       animals live

3. survive   c. to push or break through

Complete each sentence with the correct vocabulary word.

4. Without food, water, and shelter, animals

   _____

   cannot _____ .

5. A rain forest is one type of _____ .

6. Write your own sentence using one of the vocabulary words.

   _____

   _____

   _____

   _____

Around the World

SUMMARY This reader takes children around the world to explore different animals in their habitats. Children explore cause-and-effect relationships by reading about animals adapting to their surroundings. Captions provide practice for the advanced reader to use text features.

LESSON VOCABULARY

desert   forest   world

INTRODUCE THE BOOK

INTRODUCE THE TITLE AND AUTHOR Discuss the title and the author of *Around the World.* Ask children to look at the photograph on the cover and comment about the place shown in the photograph. Ask them to name the animal if they can and tell something about it.

BUILD BACKGROUND Display a globe or world map. Point to examples of the habitats and places described in the book. Ask children if there are forests, deserts, or very cold places in the United States. Ask them if there are any of these places near your community.

PREVIEW/TAKE A PICTURE WALK Have children look through the book, paying special attention to the captions. Encourage them to name the animals they can. Ask if children have seen any of the animals in other contexts, such as at a zoo or in another book. Guide them to predict what the book will be about.

READ THE BOOK

SET PURPOSE On page 3 the author invites the reader to set a purpose for reading. Help children narrow their purpose by asking what animal they would like to learn about the most. Remind children to keep their purposes in mind as they read the book.

STRATEGY SUPPORT: TEXT STRUCTURE Remind children that as they read this book, they will read about animals from different parts of the world. Ask children how the author might organize this information. Encourage children to pay attention to how the information is organized in the story.

COMPREHENSION QUESTIONS

PAGE 3 Can you predict where the polar bear lives? *(Possible response: I think it lives somewhere cold.)*

PAGE 4 How do polar bears stay warm? *(They have thick fur that keeps them warm.)*

PAGE 5 Why do walruses grab the ice with their tusks? *(to get out of the water)*

PAGE 6 Why are deserts dry? *(because deserts get very little rain)*

PAGE 9 Do you think a polar bear would like to live in a forest? Why? *(No, because it is used to the cold and ice of the North Pole)*

REVISIT THE BOOK

THINK AND SHARE

1. Possible response: Walruses make holes in the sea ice to poke their heads out of the water and breathe.
2. Possible response: It helped me remember the information.
3. pages 3 and 9
4. Possible response: Some animals live in cold places.

EXTEND UNDERSTANDING As children read the book, pause and discuss how the captions help them understand the text and photographs. When children come to pages 6 and 7, pause. Ask: Where do you think camels store their food? How do you know? What helped you find the meaning of the word *hump*?

RESPONSE OPTIONS

WRITING Assist children in writing an acrostic poem describing one of the animals. Help children prepare to write by brainstorming adjectives together.

ELL If the acrostic poem activity is too difficult, have children draw a picture and write a descriptive sentence about their favorite animals in the book.

SCIENCE CONNECTION

Students can learn more about animals of the world and in their own community. Arrange with the librarian to have books about local habitats for students to read. Help children connect their experiences with the local climate to features of the local animals.

Skill Work

TEACH/REVIEW VOCABULARY

Form small groups to create word webs. Have children put the vocabulary word *world* in the center. Then connect the words *forest* and *desert* to *world*. Ask children to look through the book for words that relate to the vocabulary words. Show them how to write their chosen words in circles extending from *forest* or *desert*.

TARGET SKILL AND STRATEGY

CAUSE AND EFFECT Review *cause-and-effect* relationships by asking children to think as they read about what is happening and why. After children have read page 4 ask: What do polar bears have? (*thick fur*) Why do they have thick fur? (*because it is so cold near the North Pole*) On the board, assist children to draw a graphic organizer that shows how the ideas are related.

TEXT STRUCTURE Share with children that *text structure* is the way information is organized in a book. Explain that sometimes the information is organized in groups by things that have something in common. Have children look at pages 4 and 5. Ask: What do these pages have in common? (*they both talk about animals that like cold places*) Repeat with pages 6 and 7.

ADDITIONAL SKILL INSTRUCTION

MAIN IDEA After reading, lead children to identify the main idea of the book by asking the following questions: What is the book about? (*animals*) What is the most important idea about this topic? (*different animals live in different places*) Do you think the author chose a good title for this book? Why or why not? Explain that by identifying the main idea of the book children can tell that they understood what they read. One way to think about the main idea is to think about a phrase that would be a good title for the book.

Name _____

Cause and Effect

Read the paragraphs from the book. Think about what happened and why it happened. Then answer the questions.

> Deserts are very dry. These places get very little rain. Animals that live in the desert need to be able to live with only a little water and food.
>
> Camels live in the desert. Camels have humps that help them store food. They do not need to find food all the time.

I. Why are most deserts very dry?

_____

_____

2. Why do animals in the desert need to live with only a little water and food?

_____

_____

3. Why don't camels need to find food all the time?

_____

_____

4. Write a sentence about something that happened to you today and why it happened. Hint: Use the word *because* in your sentence.

_____

_____

Name _____

Vocabulary

Draw a line to match the word to its meaning.

Words to Know
world   forest   desert

I. world

a. land that is very dry

2. forest

b. the Earth

3. desert

c. land with many trees and plants

Label the pictures. Use a word from the box.

4. _____

5. _____

Rules at School

SUMMARY This story is about three friends working together to follow school rules. Together they talk about why following rules is important to stay safe and be fair.

LESSON VOCABULARY

chores	cooperation
household	rules

INTRODUCE THE BOOK

INTRODUCE THE TITLE AND AUTHOR Discuss with children the title and the author of *Rules at School*. Also have children describe the characters they see on the cover. Ask: Who do you think these characters are? Where do you think they are and what are they doing? Based on the title, *Rules at School*, what do you think this book will be about?

BUILD BACKGROUND Engage children in a discussion of school rules and why they are important. Ask: What are some of our school's rules? Why do we have these rules? Why is it important to have rules? What would happen if we didn't have rules or didn't follow the rules?

PREVIEW/TAKE A PICTURE WALK Have the children preview the book, looking at the illustrations. Encourage them to describe what they see happening on each page and make predictions about the text. Ask: What are the characters doing on this page? What do you think will happen in the story? How do you think these pictures will help us understand the story?

ELL Encourage English language learners to describe in their home languages what is happening on each page. Do this as you preview the book and also during reading to aid in comprehension.

READ THE BOOK

SET PURPOSE As you preview the book, guide the children in setting a purpose for reading. Encourage children to share what interests them about the illustrations and why they want to find out what happens in the text. Say: I am curious about this picture on page 8. It looks like the characters are talking about something important. I am going to read to find out what it is.

STRATEGY SUPPORT: PREDICT AND SET PURPOSE Predicting helps children think ahead and focus on what they are reading. Remember to stop at key points to ask children what they think will happen next. Then remind them to check whether they were correct.

COMPREHENSION QUESTIONS

PAGE 4 What is page 4 all about? *(Bunny, Chip, and Scamper say they will cooperate and follow the rules.)*

PAGE 7 Scamper just cut in line for the swing. How do you think Bunny feels about this and why? What do you think she will do? *(Responses will vary: Children may predict that Bunny will be sad or angry, and she will say something to Scamper. Children's responses should include a personal statement about how they might react in the same situation.)*

PAGE 9 What does Chip say and do? Why do you think he did this? *(Chip says he is tired of waiting and pops his lunch bag. He is bored.)*

PAGE 11 Bunny says that tomorrow she and her friends should try harder to follow the rules. Do you think Bunny, Scamper, and Chip will do better tomorrow? What makes you think so? *(Responses will vary.)*

REVISIT THE BOOK

THINK AND SHARE

1. Possible pictures: Walk: Bunny runs into Chip; Take Turns: Scamper grabs the swing; Eat Quietly: Chip pops his lunch bag

2. Possible response: Yes, I predicted that she would feel bad about it because they are friends and she knows she broke a school rule.

3. Possible response: A rule tells what you should do or how to behave.

4. Possible response: Bunny, Chip, and Scamper did things without thinking about what could happen if they broke the rules.

EXTEND UNDERSTANDING Call children's attention to the illustrations on pages 3 and 4. Point out the "Chores" and "School Rules" lists in the illustrations. Discuss with children how these elements help add to the story. Ask: How do the "Chores" and "School Rules" lists help you better understand the text on the page? How do they help you better understand the rest of the story?

RESPONSE OPTIONS

WRITING Have each child write down one rule he or she thinks is important for the classroom. Invite children to share their rules and explain why they are important. During your discussion, write these rules on a large piece of paper and post it in the classroom for children to see.

ART CONNECTION

Ask children to draw pictures of themselves doing one of their chores at home, for example, cleaning their rooms, setting the table, walking the dog. Share these with the class and discuss why it is important to have chores and contribute to the family and household.

Skill Work

TEACH/REVIEW VOCABULARY

Say each of the vocabulary words with the children and ask what they think these words have in common. Discuss how we all have household chores and what those chores are. Also discuss the importance of rules (both at school and home) and cooperation. Encourage children to use the words in the context of your conversation.

TARGET SKILL AND STRATEGY

SEQUENCE Before reading, tell children to keep track of the *sequence*, or order of activities, or events, that are described. Remind them to think about what happens first, next, and last as they read.

PREDICT AND SET PURPOSE Have children look at pages 3 and 4 and then at pages 10 and 11 of the book. Ask them to describe what happened at the end of the book. Ask again what they had predicted. Ask: Were you surprised by how the friends behaved in the story? Was your prediction right? Did this make for a better story than if the friends had all followed the rules? Why?

ADDITIONAL SKILL INSTRUCTION

CHARACTER Tell children that a character is a person or animal in the story. Ask: Who are the different characters in this story? What does Scamper do in the story? When Scamper cut in line for the swing, what did you think about him? What did Scamper say after Bunny reminded him that it was not his turn? Did your feelings about Scamper change?

Name _____

Sequence

These events from *Rules at School* are out of order. Put them in the correct order by writing the numbers 1–10 next to them.

_____ 1. Chip pops his lunch bag as loud as he can.

_____ 2. Chip's clay plane falls.

_____ 3. Mrs. Pine talks to Bunny, Chip, and Scamper.

_____ 4. Scamper grabs the swing as hard as he can.

_____ 5. Bunny runs down the hall as fast as she can.

_____ 6. Scamper's new white shirt has red juice all over it.

_____ 7. Bunny waits for her turn on the swing.

_____ 8. Chip offers to help Scamper wash out the stain.

_____ 9. Bunny offers to help Chip put his plane back together.

_____ 10. Scamper offers Bunny her turn on the swing.

Name _____

Vocabulary

Pick a word from the word box that best completes each sentence.

> **Words to Know**
>
> chores   cooperation   household   rules

1. We are like a big family. Our _____ is this school.

2. We all have _____ to do.

3. We all have _____ to follow.

4. _____ means working together.

5. Write a sentence using the word **cooperation**.

_____

_____

_____

_____

_____

School: Then and Now

SUMMARY This informational book examines the early days of United States education and compares schools of the past to those of the present day.

LESSON VOCABULARY

group   respect   share

INTRODUCE THE BOOK

INTRODUCE THE TITLE AND AUTHOR Discuss with children the title and author of *School: Then and Now*. Ask children whether they think this book will be real or make-believe, and why they think so. Based on the title and the cover photograph, guide children to understand that this book compares schools of the past to present-day schools.

BUILD BACKGROUND Make a KWL chart labeled "Schools of the Past." Ask children to tell what they know about schools of the past. Show pictures from the book or other photographs to spark ideas as needed. List children's ideas in the *What We Know* column. Next, have them generate questions about the topic. List these in the *What We Want to Know* column. Return to the chart after discussion to complete the *What We Learned* column.

PREVIEW/TAKE A PICTURE WALK Lead children on a guided exploration of the book. Turn to page 3 and read the caption. Ask children to find the school bell in the photographs. Turn to pages 4 and 5 and invite children to compare the images on these pages. Ask: Which classroom looks more like our classroom? Read the caption on page 6. Think aloud: "I wonder what a hornbook is. We'll have to read and find out." Read the caption on page 8. Point out that there aren't any roads near the schoolhouse in the picture. Ask: how do you think the teachers and children got to school?

READ THE BOOK

SET PURPOSE Have children set a purpose for reading *School: Then and Now*. Suggest that they look at the KWL chart and think about what they would like to learn. Suggest that they choose one or two topics to look for as they read.

STRATEGY SUPPORT: MONITOR AND FIX UP Encourage children to think aloud as they read. If they encounter a word or a passage they do not understand, have them discuss the word or passage to decide what to do next.

COMPREHENSION QUESTIONS

PAGE 3 How does our school day begin? What is one difference between the beginning of our school day and the way school days began a long time ago? *(Possible response: We have a morning message. Back then, children had to take out their hornbooks and recite their numbers.)*

PAGE 4 What did children have to share long ago? What do we have to share today? *(Responses will vary: Long ago, children shared a classroom, a teacher, and a bench. Today we share a lunchroom.)*

PAGE 6 What do children today use instead of hornbooks? *(Possible response: Children use books and computers.)*

PAGE 7 Name some topics we study now that children didn't study a long time ago. *(Responses will vary but might mention computers or other topics.)*

REVISIT THE BOOK

THINK AND SHARE

1. Possible response: There were no machines to make cleaning and cooking easier, so children had to help with chores.
2. Possible response: By looking at a picture of a hornbook, I can see what a hornbook looked like on both sides.
3. Responses will vary but may include: In my school—many classrooms, many teachers, books, computers, paper, pencils, crayons; Long ago—one classroom, one teacher, hornbooks, benches
4. Responses will vary but could include observations about the size of the schools or the kinds of activities shown.

EXTEND UNDERSTANDING Focus children's attention on the caption on page 3. Together, think of captions for other photographs in the book. Write the captions on sticky notes and add them to the book. Then read the book with the new captions in place. Discuss whether the captions make the book easier to understand.

RESPONSE OPTIONS

WRITING Invite children to imagine that they are children in a school long ago. Have them write and illustrate a few sentences about what they might do.

SOCIAL STUDIES CONNECTION

Time For SOCIAL STUDIES

Suggest that children interview their parents, grandparents, or other older adults to find out what school was like when they were in first grade. Questions might include: How did you get to school? What did you study? Children can compile the results in a class book.

Skill Work

TEACH/REVIEW VOCABULARY

Write the word *share* on the board. Ask children what they think of when they hear the word. Write their suggestions on the board. Next, ask them to draw a picture for the word *share*. Finally, turn to page 4 and read the sentence containing the word *shared*. Discuss what the word means in this context. Repeat for *groups* (page 4) and *respect* (page 5).

TARGET SKILL AND STRATEGY

CAUSE AND EFFECT Point out to children that when they read, they can think about things that happen and why they happen. Pick up a pencil and drop it on the floor. Ask: What happened to the pencil? Why did it fall on the ground? Then help children identify an example of cause and effect as they read the text on page 8. Ask: Did children long ago have time to play with their friends after school? Why not?

MONITOR AND FIX UP Remind children that if something they are reading doesn't make sense, sometimes it helps to keep reading. Turn to page 6 and think aloud: "It says that children of long ago had hornbooks. I don't know what a hornbook is. This doesn't make sense. I should read on and find out if this word is explained."

ELL Use a Venn diagram to help English language learners compare and contrast modern schools with schools of the past.

ADDITIONAL SKILL INSTRUCTION

DRAW CONCLUSIONS Point out to children that they can use what they have read and what they know to figure out more about what happens in the book. Think aloud: "In the book, I learned that children back then had to sit on wooden benches. In our classroom, there are lots of places to sit. I think that classrooms today are more comfortable than they were a long time ago." Invite children to make their own conclusions about information in the book.

Name _____

Cause and Effect

Read each sentence.
Underline the part of the sentence that tells *what happened*.
Circle the part of the sentence that tells *why it happened*.

Example:

Most children walked to school because they had no cars.

1. The children went inside because they heard the school bell.

2. When the teacher said, "It's time to study the alphabet,"
   the children got out their hornbooks.

3. Because the children had to do chores, they couldn't play
   after school.

4. Draw pictures in the boxes.

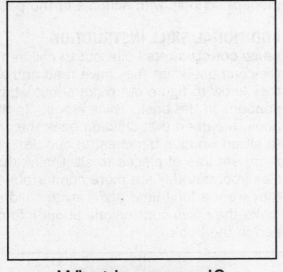

What happened?

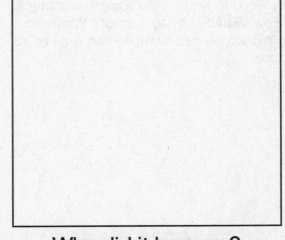

Why did it happen?

Name _____

Vocabulary

Choose a word from the box to complete each sentence.

Words to Know

| group | respect | share |

1. In school, it is important to _____ the rules of the classroom.

2. The girls sat on the floor in a _____ .

3. They had to _____ their art supplies with the boys.

Draw a picture to show these words.

group   share

Mom the Mayor

SUMMARY Through letter format, Ramon tells Carlos about his mother's job as mayor of their community. We learn that the mayor's job begins early in the morning. Mayor Martinez then meets with people in the community to discuss how to make it an even better place. Ramon ends by saying that his mom is a good mayor, but an even better mom.

LESSON VOCABULARY

citizen	community
law	leader

INTRODUCE THE BOOK

INTRODUCE THE TITLE AND AUTHOR Point to the book title, and read it with the class. Then point to the author's name, and read it too. Ask children to consider what *Mom the Mayor* might mean. Confirm for children that this book is about a mayor who is also a mother.

BUILD BACKGROUND Encourage children to share their ideas about a mayor's job. Then inform children that a mayor is the leader of a community. A mayor listens to people in the community to solve problems and to find ways to make the community even better. Speculate with children what tasks the mayor in this book might do.

PREVIEW/TAKE A PICTURE WALK

Have children look through the book to notice interesting things about it. For example, on page 3, have children study the text and identify the genre. *(It is a letter.)* Then ask children who the woman in the picture might be, and confirm that she is the mayor. Encourage children to look through the book to find other pictures of Mayor Mom.

ELL Write each word slowly on the board as you say it out loud. Then run your finger below each word, say the word, and have children say it with you. Next to each word, write words children know to help them make connections, for example: *community = neighborhood; leader = mayor; citizen = person; law = rule.*

READ THE BOOK

SET PURPOSE Remind children that when they set a purpose for reading, they think about what they would like to learn. Encourage children to set a purpose for reading this book, for example, perhaps they want to learn why the mayor is called Mayor Mom. Tell children to look for the answer as they read.

STRATEGY SUPPORT: IMPORTANT IDEAS Remind children that important ideas are facts and details that tell more about the main idea of the story. Model finding an important idea on page 3: I read that the mom's day at the office starts at eight o'clock. I know that this story is mostly about the mom's new job as mayor, and this sentence tells me more about it. This is an important idea.

COMPREHENSION QUESTIONS

PAGE 4 Why does the author include a picture of a group of people, along with a picture of Mayor Mom? *(to show the people in the community that Mayor Mom meets with)*

PAGE 5 What question can help you understand these photographs? *(Why is there a letter pictured?)*

PAGE 8 How is the picture of the merry-go-round related to the mayor's job? *(That ride was at the town's festival. The mayor can work to have another festival.)*

PAGE 9 How do you think Ramon feels about his mom? *(He is proud of her. He thinks it is neat that she's the mayor. He admires her for working so hard and helping people.)*

REVISIT THE BOOK

THINK AND SHARE

1. Possible response: The author wants readers to learn about the mayor's day, from start to finish.

2. Responses will vary.

3. Possible response: A law is a rule made by the government that all people need to follow.

4. Possible response: The clocks tell us when the mayor does different activities throughout the day.

EXTEND UNDERSTANDING Point out the planner on page 11. Have children copy the planner onto another sheet of paper. Instruct children to erase the times on the planner and to replace them with the times they see on the clocks in the book. Then encourage children to fill in the planner so that the planner summarizes the mayor's day.

RESPONSE OPTIONS

WRITING Recall with children that this book features a letter in which one child tells a friend what his mother does. Invite children to choose someone in their family or neighborhood that they could write a letter about. Have them write their letters, describing what the person does in a day.

LISTENING AND SPEAKING Share with children that when people want to become mayor, they give speeches that explain their ideas for the community. Encourage children to suggest things they might say in a speech if they wanted to become mayor. Ask the rest of the class to listen to their classmates' ideas, then add ideas of their own.

SOCIAL STUDIES CONNECTION

Time For SOCIAL STUDIES

Share with children the name(s) of the mayor(s) of their towns or communities. You might call your municipal center to see if they have a biography available about the mayor. You might also inquire if the mayor has time to make school visits.

Skill Work

TEACH/REVIEW VOCABULARY

Begin sentences with each vocabulary word, and challenge students to complete each sentence with a brief example or explanation. For example: A community is _____. A leader is _____. A law is _____. A citizen is _____.

TARGET SKILL AND STRATEGY

⊙ **AUTHOR'S PURPOSE** Remind children that the *author's purpose* is the reason why an author chose to write a story. Speculate why an author might choose to write a book called *Mayor Mom. (The author wanted to explain the job of a mayor.)* Recognizing the author's purpose helps readers grasp a book's content.

⊙ **IMPORTANT IDEAS** Explain that *important ideas* tell more about the main idea of the story. Ask: What important ideas did you read in this story? How do you know they are important?

ADDITIONAL SKILL INSTRUCTION

CAUSE/EFFECT Explain to children that sometimes things that happen in a book cause other things to happen. Help children make the connection that one action can cause something else to happen; this is called cause and effect. Then help children recognize a cause-and-effect situation in the book. Have children turn to page 6, and ask, "What caused this playground to be built?" Have children read the text to find the cause: A boy wrote a letter to Mayor Mom asking for a new playground, and Mayor Mom met with community leaders to discuss it.

Name _____

Author's Purpose

Read the letter below. Answer the questions.

Dear Carlos,

My mom is the new mayor of our town! I'm sending you pictures, and I want to tell you about her job.

Here's my mom at work. Her day at the office starts at eight o'clock.

Mom has many things to do every day. She checks her schedule each morning when she gets to work. These are some of the people she will meet with this week. Mom works hard at her job.

Your friend,

Ramon

I. Why do you think the author wrote this story in the form of a letter?

_____

_____

_____

2. Why do you think Ramon tells Carlos about his mom?

_____

_____

_____

Name _____

Vocabulary

Write the correct word from the box to complete each sentence.

Words to Know

citizen   community   law   leader

_____

1. A _____ is like a rule that everyone must follow.

_____

2. A _____ is a person in charge, like a mayor.

_____

3. A _____ is a person who lives in a country legally.

_____

4. A _____ is a kind of neighborhood.

The Dinosaur Detectives

SUMMARY Dinosaurs had a variety of ways to protect themselves from enemies. These ways included protective body features, ways of fighting, and living in herds.

LESSON VOCABULARY

enemy   extinct

protect

INTRODUCE THE BOOK

INTRODUCE THE TITLE AND AUTHOR Discuss with children the title and author of *The Dinosaur Detectives*. Lead them to define *detective* *(someone who tries to solve mysteries)*. Based on the title, what do the children think the book will be about?

BUILD BACKGROUND Have children share what they know about dinosaurs. Ask them to think of and discuss ways in which dinosaurs might have protected themselves. Let children know that they will be learning more about how dinosaurs protected themselves.

PREVIEW/TAKE A PICTURE WALK Invite children to look at the pictures in the book. Point out the captions and labels that tell the names of the dinosaurs, and information about the protective parts of a dinosaur's body.

READ THE BOOK

SET PURPOSE Have children set a purpose for reading *The Dinosaur Detectives*. Revisit what children already know about dinosaurs. Then discuss what further information they hope to learn about dinosaurs.

STRATEGY SUPPORT: INFERRING Remind children that they can use what's in the text to make a guess about something the author didn't say. Model making an inference on page 5: The text says that the stegosaurus protected itself by swinging its tail back and forth. I know that some dinosaurs attacked other dinosaurs. I think the stegosaurus had this special feature to protect itself from other dinosaurs. It could injure the dinosaurs with the spikes on its tail.

COMPREHENSION QUESTIONS

PAGE 3 When did dinosaurs live? *(millions of years ago)*

PAGE 5 How did a stegosaurus most likely protect itself from enemies? *(It swung its long spiky tail. It had bony plates on its back.)*

PAGE 6 How did an apatosaurus most likely protect itself from enemies? *(Its size might have frightened off other animals and it might have used its long tail to fight.)*

PAGE 7 What is one way to better understand what the author means by *The triceratops had three large horns? (Possible response: Look at the illustration.)*

PAGE 8 How did an allosaurus's mouth help keep it safe? *(It had a large jaw and long, sharp teeth.)*

REVIST THE BOOK

THINK AND SHARE

1. First: stegosaurus; Next: apatosaurus; Then: triceratops; Last: allosaurus
2. Possible response: The triceratops probably used its horns to charge at other animals. This guess helps me understand that all dinosaurs had special features such as sharp horns for a reason.
3. It should be clear that children understand it means to "no longer exist."
4. Its teeth and claws are labeled. Non-labeled parts will vary but may include neck, legs, and head.

EXTEND UNDERSTANDING Ask children if they looked at the illustrations before reading the information on each page, during reading, or after reading. Discuss how the illustrations helped them to better understand what they were reading about dinosaurs.

RESPONSE OPTIONS

WRITING Ask children to imagine they are one of the dinosaurs they just read about. Then, have them write a paragraph describing how life would be for themselves from the point of view of that dinosaur.

SCIENCE CONNECTION

Display books that show a variety of dinosaur fossils. Encourage children to try and figure out information about the dinosaurs by looking at the fossils. Then suggest that they check the rest of the information in the book to see if they were correct.

Skill Work

TEACH/REVIEW VOCABULARY

Have children take turns giving the definition of a vocabulary word while other children guess the word that is being defined.

ELL To check for understanding, invite children to retell the sections of information in their own words.

TARGET SKILL AND STRATEGY

SEQUENCE Tell children that a good way to understand information in a book is to be clear about the order in which events happen. Discuss that people know about dinosaurs through the study of fossils. Have children put the following events in order: People find fossils. *(3)* People get information about animals by looking at fossils. *(4)* Animals become fossils. *(2)* An animal dies. *(1)*

INFERRING To *infer* is to use background knowledge and what's in the text to make a guess about something the author didn't say. As children read, encourage them to make inferences whenever possible. Explain that good readers connect text to what they already know in order to understand the story better.

ADDITIONAL SKILL INSTRUCTION

DRAW CONCLUSIONS Discuss that when children read, they should use the words and pictures in the book, as well their own knowledge to make decisions about what they are reading. As children read *The Dinosaur Detectives*, have them think about what decisions or opinions they are making about dinosaurs. Afterwards, have children discuss these decisions.

Name _____

Sequence

Reread page 3 of *The Dinosaur Detectives*. Use the boxes below to make a picture story of what you learned on that page. Put one event in each box. Under each picture, write a caption for your picture.

1.

_____

- - - - - - - - - - - - - - - - - - - -

_____

2.

_____

- - - - - - - - - - - - - - - - - - - -

_____

3.

_____

- - - - - - - - - - - - - - - - - - - -

_____

4.

_____

- - - - - - - - - - - - - - - - - - - -

_____

Name _____

Vocabulary

Use the vocabulary words to fill in the blanks in the sentences.
Then, write a sentence of your own using one of the words.

Words to Know

enemy	extinct	protect

1. The allosaurus was an _____ of many dinosaurs.

2. A stegosaurus could _____ itself with its spiky tail.

3. Today dinosaurs are _____ .

4. _____

All About Food Chains

🔹 **AUTHOR'S PURPOSE/POINT OF VIEW**
🔹 **BACKGROUND KNOWLEDGE**

SUMMARY This book explores the relationship between plants and animals in a food chain, stressing that when one link is lost, the food chain is broken. As an example, readers learn about life in a forest where snakes eat grasshoppers and grasshoppers eat grass.

LESSON VOCABULARY
environment
require
thrive

INTRODUCE THE BOOK

INTRODUCE THE TITLE AND AUTHOR Prompt children to express their reactions to the book cover, eliciting ideas about the snake and the grasshopper. Then read the title and author name with them. Encourage discussion about what a food chain might be. Ask: Do you see any "links" in a food chain on this cover?

BUILD BACKGROUND Invite children to look out the classroom window and to identify things in nature that they see, such as the sun, trees, a grassy field. Tell children that the sun helps plants grow. Animals eat plants, and animals eat other animals. Explain that this chain of events is called the *food chain.*

PREVIEW Work with children to explore the photographs and graphic elements in the book. Look at page 3 and ask children to describe the pictures. Have children finger-trace the dashed lines, and help them realize that these lines represent a chain that links the pictures together. Encourage children to finger-trace the lines and arrows that connect pictures on following pages too.

READ THE BOOK

SET PURPOSE Elicit from children why they might like to read this book, and encourage them to set their own purpose for reading. For example, children might say they'd like to learn more about the snake on the cover or learn what a food chain is. Encourage children to look for the snake or the food chain when they read.

STRATEGY SUPPORT: BACKGKROUND KNOWLEDGE Remind children that they can use what they already know to understand the story better. As children finish reading page 3, pause and model how to connect the text to their background knowledge. Say: This reminds me of when I saw a bird eating a worm. The worm is food for the bird. The food gives the bird energy. Have you ever seen a living thing get its food?

COMPREHENSION QUESTIONS

PAGE 4 Why does the author include the sun in a discussion about food chains? (*Possible response: All food chains begin with the sun, which plants need to thrive.*)

PAGES 6–7 What words might we read on these pages, based on the photographs? (*Possible response: snake, grass, grasshopper*)

PAGE 9 How are plants and people linked? (*Possible response: people take care of plants, and plants grow. People eat the plants.*)

REVISIT THE BOOK

THINK AND SHARE

1. Possible response: The author wrote about the food chain first so that readers understand the subject.
2. Possible response: I already knew that some animals eat plants and some animals eat other animals. This helped me understand why certain animals were lower on the food chain.
3. Possible response: *grow, flourish, prosper, blossom, succeed, develop*
4. Possible response: Both diagrams show the same food chain. The diagram on page 8 shows what happens if the chain is broken.

EXTEND UNDERSTANDING Have children turn to pages 10 and 11 in the book and explore the chart on the page 10. Discuss how the chart reflects ideas in the text and confirm that it identifies plants and animals. Ask children why they think the author might have included this activity. For example: The author wants kids to become more aware of the plants and animals around them.

RESPONSE OPTIONS

WRITING Invite children to write captions for each of the pictures on pages 4 and 5. In their sentences, challenge children to explain how the pictures are related or linked in the food chain.

SCIENCE CONNECTION

Work with children to think of a food chain that occurs in their area. For example, trees produce nuts; nuts are food for squirrels. Have children illustrate their own food chains, using paper plates for each "food."

Skill Work

TEACH/REVIEW VOCABULARY

Write each word on the board, saying it out loud. Call attention to the number of syllables in each word, having children count the syllables as they say the word. Then talk about the meaning of the word.

ELL Introduce words children might already know, then build upon this knowledge with the vocabulary words: *need = require; grow = thrive; nature = environment.* Ask: What other words do you know that relate to the vocabulary words?

TARGET SKILL AND STRATEGY

AUTHOR'S PURPOSE/POINT OF VIEW Explain that the *author's purpose* is the reason why an author chose to write something. Read the first paragraph with the group. Ask children why the author mentions that people are living things too. For example, the author might want us to recognize that we are also part of a food chain. This is probably what the author believes, which is the author's point of view.

BACKGROUND KNOWLEDGE Review with children that *background knowledge* can come from their own experiences, from reading, and from things other people have taught them. Background knowledge can help them understand what they are reading. As children read, encourage them to use their background knowledge whenever possible.

ADDITIONAL SKILL INSTRUCTION

CAUSE AND EFFECT Write the words *cause* and *effect* on the board. Set up a tower of blocks on the floor. Roll a ball along the floor so that it knocks over the blocks. Invite children to describe what has happened. Identify their ideas as cause and effect:

1. The rolling ball caused something to happen.

2. The falling blocks are the effect of the rolling ball.

Have children turn to page 8 and diagram a scenario that explains a cause and effect. Cause: no more grasshoppers ⟶ Effect: snakes die

Name _____

Author's Purpose/Point of View

Read the sentences below.

A food chain happens when one living thing eats another.

Food chains are found in every environment.

They are alike in an important way.

Food chains begin with the sun and plants.

Plants use the energy from the sun to make food.

When an animal eats a plant's leaves, the plant's energy passes to the animal.

Why do you think the author wrote these sentences?

Use the words in the box to fill in the blanks.

energy living food chains

1. The author cares about _____ things.

2. The author wants to show that _____ from the sun helps plants make food.

3. The author wants to talk about _____ .

Name _____

Vocabulary

Read the sentences. Think about the underlined word.
What does it mean? Write the meaning on the lines.

1. Plants, animals, the soil, water, and the sun are all part of the <u>environment</u>.

_____
- -
_____
- -
_____.

2. All living things on Earth <u>require</u> the sun's energy to live.

_____
- -
_____
- -
_____.

3. Plants and animals <u>thrive</u> when they get the proper food and water.

_____
- -
_____
- -
_____.

Bees and
Beekeepers

SUMMARY People who raise and work with bees are called beekeepers. A beekeeper maintains the hive, cares for the bees, and extracts the honey and wax from the hive for people to use.

LESSON VOCABULARY
individual
industrious
special

INTRODUCE THE BOOK

INTRODUCE THE TITLE AND AUTHOR Invite children to explore the cover of this book. First prompt them to react to the outfit worn by the person on the cover, then help them notice the bees in the photograph. Speculate why the outfit might be important and who this person might be. Then read the title and author name with the group. Help children recognize the smaller word *bee* in *beekeeper*. Ask: What do you think a beekeeper does?

BUILD BACKGROUND Remind children that honey is found inside a beehive. Explain that beekeepers raise bees in order to produce honey. Ask: Would you like to be a beekeeper? Why, or why not?

PREVIEW/TAKE A PICTURE WALK Encourage children to preview the pictures and text. Allow children to respond to the pictures that show the beekeeper in close range of the bees. Point out the text on pages 4 and 5, and ask children to explain the difference between the dark text and the red text. Make sure children recognize the red text as photo captions.

READ THE BOOK

SET PURPOSE Encourage children to think about why they might like to read this book. Elicit ideas, such as "Why are beekeepers needed?" Tell children to look for the answers to their questions as they read.

STRATEGY SUPPORT: QUESTIONING Tell children that stopping and asking questions as they read can help them make sure they understand the information. Model this strategy of page 4: As I read this page, I wonder why the boxes open at the top and at the bottom. I will write this question down on a sticky note and attach it to this page. At the end of the story, I'll come back to this page and see if I can answer the question then.

COMPREHENSION QUESTIONS

PAGE 3 What is the difference between beekeepers and people who don't like bees? *(Many people who don't like bees are afraid of them; beekeepers are not afraid of bees.)*

PAGE 5 Why does the beekeeper give the bees medicine? *(to help them stay well)*

PAGE 7 What are the sentences on this page all about? *(the queen bee and drones)*

PAGE 8 What two things do beekeepers get from a honeycomb? *(honey and wax)*

REVISIT THE BOOK

THINK AND SHARE

1. Alike: All are bees. They all live in the hive. A beekeeper takes care of them. Different: Queen bees lay eggs. Worker bees do other jobs.
2. Responses will vary.
3. Responses will vary.
4. Possible response: I learned that a group of bees is called a colony. The colony lives in a hive.

EXTEND UNDERSTANDING Point out to children that the book does not provide specific information about the beekeeper's suit. Read the activity on pages 10 and 11 with the group, and talk about how children can find additional information about this equipment. Have children predict how the suit might help the beekeeper, then help children conduct research to confirm ideas and form new ones.

RESPONSE OPTIONS

WRITING Ask children if they have any additional questions for the beekeeper that were not answered in the book. Have children write their questions. If time and resources allow, encourage children to research and write the answers.

WORD WORK Remind children of the phrase *busy as a bee*. Ask children if they have a better understanding of the phrase, and talk about the meaning of the phrase and how it relates to bees. Say the phrase *industrious as a bee*, and ask children if it has the same impact as *busy as a bee*. Let children explain why or why not. Point out that the words people choose can impact the meaning or tone.

SCIENCE CONNECTION

Prompt children to imagine that they live next to someone who is a beekeeper. Speculate with children how their outdoor environment might change. Ask children if they would like to live next to a beekeeper and to explain why or why not.

Skill Work

TEACH/REVIEW VOCABULARY

Say each word for the class, then invite children to say the words with you. Write each word on the chalkboard, and help children recognize their separate sounds. Then discuss the meaning of each word.

ELL Say the word *individual,* and hold up one finger. Have children repeat the word and your action. Say the word *industrious,* and pantomime doing a lot of things. Have children repeat. Encourage children to practice saying these words so they become familiar with their sounds.

TARGET SKILL AND STRATEGY

COMPARE AND CONTRAST Share with children that when they say how two things are *alike,* they tell how they are the same. When they say how two things are *different,* they tell how they are not the same. Have children discuss how bees in the wild and bees raised by people are similar. *(They live in hives. They have many jobs.)* Discuss how the bees are different. *(Bees raised by people do not build their own hives. Bees raised by people may get food and medicine from people.)*

QUESTIONING Ask: What questions did you have as you read *Bees and Beekeepers*? Did reading on in the text help to answer your questions? Where else might you find the answer? Lead children to understand that they can use encyclopedias and online sources if they still have questions about a nonfiction text.

ADDITIONAL SKILL INSTRUCTION

MAIN IDEA After children have finished reading the book, ask: What was the selection *Bees and Beekeepers* about? Give children three choices: Is it about what bees do? Is it about how honey is made? Is it about what beekeepers do? Confirm that the main idea is the work that a beekeeper does. Have children reread the book and start a word web to record details that support the main idea. Title the center circle "Beekeepers."

Name _____

Compare and Contrast

Fill in the diagram below. Write two facts about wild bees, then write one fact about how wild bees and beekeeper bees are the same. Write two facts about beekeeper bees.

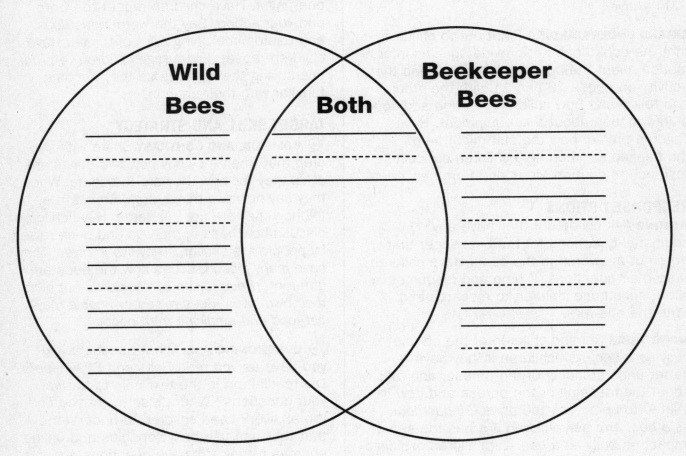

Name _____

Vocabulary

Read the paragraph below. Think about the words in dark letters.

Bees that live in a **special** hive built by a beekeeper are like bees that live in the wild. Most of them are worker bees. These **industrious** bees do many jobs around the hive. There is one **individual** queen bee. She is the only bee that lays eggs. There are also drones that help make new bees.

1. What does the word special mean?

_____

_____

_____

_____

2. What does the word industrious mean?

_____

_____

_____

_____

3. What does the word individual mean?

_____

_____

_____

_____

A New Library

SUMMARY The town has grown and needs a new library. This narrative nonfiction book tells and shows how a new library is built.

LESSON VOCABULARY

growth	makeshift
population	public
spindly	

INTRODUCE THE BOOK

INTRODUCE THE TITLE AND AUTHOR Discuss with children the title and the author of *A New Library*. Ask: Based on the title, what do you expect to learn about in this book? What are the jobs of the author and illustrator?

BUILD BACKGROUND Discuss some of the ways that towns and libraries change as they grow. Ask children to name ways that their town and library are changing.

PREVIEW As children preview the book, have them pay close attention to the illustrations and captions. Point out that reading captions is a quick way to see what information a book contains.

READ THE BOOK

SET PURPOSE Have children set a purpose for reading *A New Library*. Suggest that children look at the cover and think about what they might learn in this book. Think aloud: I would like to learn more about how a new library is built. I see pictures that show this. I'm going to read and find out more.

STRATEGY SUPPORT: SUMMARIZE Understanding the plot structure of a story can help children summarize a story. As children summarize the book, remind them to think about what happened first, next, and last.

COMPREHENSION QUESTIONS

PAGE 4 What do you predict will be the next step after people move out the library's books? (*The old library will be torn down.*)

PAGE 5 What do you think this book will tell you? (*how a new library will be built*) What gives you clues to make you think that? (*We have seen workmen tearing down the old building and digging a new foundation.*)

PAGES 6–7 What does the book tell you about the difference between the "sheets" shown on page 6 and on page 7? (*Page 6 sheets are steel; page 7 sheets are wood.*) Which sheets are used for support? (*sheets of steel on page 6*)

PAGE 8 Why do these workers do their jobs after the outside workers did their jobs? (*The outside of the building needed to be built first; inside workers finish up the job.*)

PAGE 9 What are two reasons people in the town are happy about their new library? (*It is taller so it can hold more books and computers; more people can visit to read or say hi.*)

REVISIT THE BOOK

THINK AND SHARE

1. First box: take down the old building; Middle box: dig a hole and make a strong foundation; Last box: build a frame.
2. Possible Response: This story is about a town building a new library. It tells the steps the town took to build their new large library.
3. *Public means* "belonging to everyone." Sentences will vary.
4. Responses will vary. Guide discussion to genres of books (picture books, chapter books, fairy tales, and so forth).

EXTEND UNDERSTANDING As children read, draw attention to the captions. Ask: Does the caption tell you something more about the topic? Does it help explain the illustration? Challenge children to think of a caption for the illustration on page 9.

RESPONSE OPTIONS

WRITING Have students write a sentence or two about why libraries are important.

SOCIAL STUDIES CONNECTION

Time For **SOCIAL STUDIES**

Discuss with children their nearest public library and whether they have visited it. You might consider a field trip if possible. Tell children that free public libraries are an important part of the history of the United States.

Skill Work

TEACH/REVIEW VOCABULARY

Display the word *makeshift* in a pocket chart. Read the word aloud. Then have children find the word on page 3. Have them read the sentence aloud. Ask: What is another word for makeshift? Ask children to think of another situation where they might see this word. Repeat for the other words on the list.

ELL Point out to Spanish-speaking children that the English word *public* is similar to the Spanish word *publico.*

TARGET SKILL AND STRATEGY

SEQUENCE Point out to children that this story is told in the order it which it happens. Explain that telling a story in order is a good way to better understand happens. You might set up a chart to record the order of events in *A New Library.* First, the old building is torn down. Next, a new foundation is dug. Then the outside and inside of the new building are constructed. Last, the new library is complete.

SUMMARIZE Point out that a summary of a story is a short description of the story's characters and main ideas. A summary answers the questions *Who?* and *What happens?* Encourage children to ask what the main idea of the book is as they read.

ADDITIONAL SKILL INSTRUCTION

AUTHOR'S PURPOSE Ask children why they think the author wrote this book. Point out that there may be two purposes—to explain how a building is built and to tell how important a library is to a community. Both are worthwhile purposes. Discuss the various activities people can pursue inside a library besides reading.

Name _____

Sequence

Look back through *A New Library*. Use the boxes below to draw a picture story of what happened. Draw the events in order in the boxes. Under each picture, write a caption.

I.	**2.**
_____	_____
3.	**4.**
_____	_____

Name _____

Vocabulary

Pick a word from the box to finish each sentence. Write the words on the line.

Words to Know

growth   makeshift   population
public   spindly

---

1. Our town's _____ is the largest in the state.

2. In the United States, every town has a _____ library.

3. When we moved to a new town, we stayed in a _____ _____ place until we found a new home.

4. Steel beams may look _____, but they are very strong.

5. The _____ of the town happened when people found gold there.

Paul's Bed

SUMMARY In this tall tale, it isn't easy to find a bed big enough for the fast-growing baby Paul Bunyan. A time line at the end of the book outlines the main plot events.

LESSON VOCABULARY

attempt   event   time line

INTRODUCE THE BOOK

INTRODUCE THE TITLE AND AUTHOR Discuss with children the title and the author of *Paul's Bed*. Encourage children to look closely at the cover illustration. Ask: Which character is Paul? How can you tell? Is he in a bed? Why not?

BUILD BACKGROUND Explain to children that they will be reading a tall tale, a funny story full of exaggerations. Ask them to name examples of exaggeration from stories they have read or from their own experiences.

PREVIEW As children preview the book, encourage them to examine the illustrations. Ask: Based on the illustrations, what do you think might happen in this story?

READ THE BOOK

SET PURPOSE Have children set a purpose for reading *Paul's Bed*. Suggest that children think about how they might describe this story to a friend who hasn't read it.

STRATEGY SUPPORT: INFERRING Point out that making an inference means using information from the book to make a guess about something the author didn't tell you. Remind children that they should find information in the book and then form an idea based on what they read. Have children make an inference about Paul. What inference can they make and why?

COMPREHENSION QUESTIONS

PAGE 4 The author describes Paul as "an amazing baby." What was so special about him? *(Answers will vary but should refer to Paul's size or rate of growth).*

PAGES 8-9 What are some examples of exaggeration on these pages? *(Possible responses: Paul slept in a ship; there weren't enough blankets to cover him; he was too big to fit in a cabin.)*

PAGE 14 Tell about some of the different beds that Paul used in this story. *(Paul's beds included his parents' bed, a rowboat, a ship, and a giant bed.)*

PAGE 15 What did Paul need in this story? How did he get it? *(Paul needed a bed that fit him. His parents and neighbors built him a ship to use for a bed, and as he grew bigger, he built one for himself.)*

REVISIT THE BOOK

THINK AND SHARE

1. Paul: huge baby, had a ship bed, used a quilt made of sails, was the biggest lumberjack of all; His parents: normal adult size, built a ship bed for Paul, made a huge blanket to keep Paul warm; Both: they are family

2. Possible response: Paul will build the biggest cabin in all the land. That guess helps me understand the story because Paul was too young to find a place to sleep earlier in the book. At age 16, he was old enough to build his own place to sleep.

3. A time line is a chart showing events arranged in order. This time line shows what happens to Paul as he grows.

4. Responses will vary but should recount a personal, specific episode.

EXTEND UNDERSTANDING As children discuss *A Bed for Paul*, encourage them to think about the story from Paul Bunyan's perspective. Ask: What would be good about being a giant? What would be bad?

RESPONSE OPTIONS

WRITING Invite children to make up a brief tall tale about when they were babies. Remind them to use humor and exaggeration in their stories. Encourage the children to share their stories with their classmates.

SOCIAL STUDIES CONNECTION

Time For SOCIAL STUDIES

Have children use the Internet, books, and magazines to learn more about the history of lumberjacks.

Skill Work

TEACH/REVIEW VOCABULARY

Write the word *attempt* on the board. Ask children if they know what this word means. Model how to look up the word in a children's dictionary. Ask a volunteer to read the definition aloud. Together, brainstorm a sentence using the vocabulary word. Repeat for the remaining words on the list.

ELL Print the vocabulary words on word cards. Have children choose partners. Give each pair of children a word card and challenge them to work together to find their words somewhere in the classroom. They might look in other books, in newspapers, and so forth. Have the children share their findings with their classmates.

TARGET SKILL AND STRATEGY

COMPARE AND CONTRAST Remind children that one way to understand what they are reading is to compare and contrast. Remembering information in this way can help us better understand what we read. Have children compare and contrast Paul at the beginning of the story and Paul at the end of the story. Tell them that good readers compare and contrast as they read to make sense of the text.

INFERRING Encourage children to use their knowledge to make an inference about Paul's neighbors. Help them think about Paul's neighbors and make a guess based on the information in the story. Ask children why they made their conclusion about Paul's neighbors. Have them use the illustrations and text in the book to help explain their reasoning.

ADDITIONAL SKILL INSTRUCTION

CHARACTER Remind students that a character is a person or animal who takes part in the events of a story. Explain that writers let readers know what characters are like by telling what characters do and feel. Challenge children, as they read, to look for things that Paul does, says, or feels. Invite them to use these examples to talk about what Paul is like.

Name _____

Compare and Contrast

1-4. Compare and contrast the pictures of Paul on page 15 of *Paul's Bed*. Write two ways they are alike and two ways they are different.

Paul

Alike
_____
- - - - - - - - - - - - - - - -
_____
_____
_____
_____
- - - - - - - - - - - - - - - -
_____

Different
_____
- - - - - - - - - - - - - - - -
_____
_____
_____
_____
- - - - - - - - - - - - - - - -
_____

5. Write a sentence that tells how you feel about Paul's beds.

_____
- -
_____
_____
- -
_____

Name _____

Vocabulary

Write the first letter of each picture. Read the word.

> ## Words to Know
>
> attempt   event   time line

1.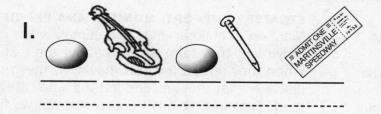

_____ _____ _____ _____ _____

_____ _____ _____ _____ _____

2.

_____ _____ _____ _____ _____ _____

_____ _____ _____ _____ _____ _____

3.

_____ _____ _____   _____ _____ _____

- - - - - - - - - -   - - - - - - - - - -

4. Write a sentence using one of the vocabulary words.

_____

_____

_____

Britton Finds a Kitten

SUMMARY A boy named Britton finds a kitten under a car. His father lets him keep the kitten and teaches him how to take care of the kitten.

LESSON VOCABULARY

mature   natural   features

INTRODUCE THE BOOK

INTRODUCE THE TITLE AND AUTHOR Display the cover and ask children to identify the animal under the car. What is happening on the cover? Conclude with children that the animal is a kitten or a cat. Invite a volunteer to point to the word *kitten*, and then read the book title with the group, as well as the author's and illustrator's names.

BUILD BACKGROUND Have children describe the pets they may have. Discuss with children where they got their pet. Explain that some pets come from a pet store, others come from a shelter, and sometimes we might get a pet from a friend whose pet had babies. Then have children name a pet and tell its characteristics. For example, a cat has soft fur.

PREVIEW/TAKE A PICTURE WALK Invite children to look through the book to become familiar with the text and the illustrations. Ask children to identify the items Britton is collecting on page 4 (*the shoe box, pillowcase, and tuna*) Speculate with children why these items might be important to the story, and list their ideas. Have children tell where they have seen Britton with these items.

READ THE BOOK

SET PURPOSE Encourage children to explain why they might like to read this book. For example, perhaps children want to discover what they need to have a kitten for a pet. Tell children to look for the answer as they read.

STRATEGY SUPPORT: MONITOR AND CLARIFY Mention to children that sometimes when they read, they form an idea about the text. When they reread the text, however, they may discover that they misunderstood what they read. Explain that it is important, then, to fix their understanding. To demonstrate what you mean, model reading page 8 and summarizing what you think you've learned. (*The vet checks your pet to make sure it is healthy.*) Then read page 7 and clarify your initial idea. (*The vet checks that your pet is healthy, and the vet teaches you how to take care of your pet.*)

COMPREHENSION QUESTIONS

PAGE 3 How might the book's title relate to the story's theme? (*The theme involves taking care of a pet, and the title tells how a boy finds a pet.*)

PAGE 7 Why was it a good idea for Britton to visit a vet with his kitten? (*The vet will teach him how to take care of his kitten and tell him whether the kitten is healthy.*)

PAGE 9 How did Britton decide on the name Patches? (*He thought of Patches because the kitten has patches of orange fur.*)

PAGE 11 What happened to Patches bed? (*She outgrew her shoebox bed, so now she sleeps with Britton in his bed.*)

REVIST THE BOOK

THINK AND SHARE

1. Facts: Kittens need something to scratch. Kittens need kitten food to eat. Opinions: Kittens love tuna fish. Patches is a great pet!
2. kitten food—to eat; a shoebox—for a bed; a pillowcase—to sleep with; toys—to play with and scratch
3. orange; Some cats have orange fur. small; Kittens are small baby cats. shy; At first, Patches was shy around Britton.
4. They change because a kitten becomes a cat. It grows from a baby cat to an adult cat. As adult cats grow, they need adult cat food and a bigger bed to sleep in. Like Britton's kitten, adult cats can grow out of the beds they used as kittens.

EXTEND UNDERSTANDING Read with children the text on page 15. Have children apply what they learn in the text to Patches in the story. (Patches grew bigger in the story. She got so big that she didn't fit in her bed and needed a new place to sleep.) Also help children explore how Britton might have felt about Patches sleeping on his bed.

RESPONSE OPTIONS

WRITING Encourage children to write letters to an animal shelter asking about the kinds of pets they have. Ask children to think about what pet they would like. In the letter, have children explain the kind of pet they are looking for.

SPEAKING Suggest to children that they have just gotten a new pet. What would they tell new friends about their pets? Have children introduce their new pets to a partner.

SOCIAL STUDIES CONNECTION

Have children use the Internet to look for animal shelters near their school or town. Have them find information about a shelter including the name of the shelter, what pets it has, and what people can do to help the shelter.

Skill Work

TEACH/REVIEW VOCABULARY

Divide children into groups and assign one vocabulary word to each group. Have children use the glossary to find the definition and then share the definition with the class. Then have each member of the group use the word in a sentence.

ELL Ask English learners to skim the story and write down any unfamiliar words. Help them by providing definitions for each word. Use the word in a sentence to further explain its meaning.

TARGET SKILL AND STRATEGY

FACT AND OPINION Help children understand the difference between facts and opinions. Facts are ideas you can prove to be true. Opinions are ideas that people think but cannot prove. Ask children to look at page 7. The sentence *A vet is a doctor for animals* is a fact. We can look in a dictionary to find the definition and prove it is true. Have children look at page 15. The sentence *Patches is a great pet* is an opinion. This is only Britton's judgment of belief.

MONITOR AND CLARIFY Instruct children to pause after they read each page and to consider what has happened so far in the story. To make sure they have understood everything correctly, tell children to reread the page and to revise, or clarify, any misunderstandings.

ADDITIONAL SKILL INSTRUCTION

SETTING Review with children that as they read, they should think about when and where the story happens. Encourage children to identify where this story happens. (*It happens in Britton's town.*) Then discuss with children why the setting of this story is important.

Name _____

Fact and Opinion

A **fact** is a piece of information that can be proven to be true. An **opinion** is a piece of information that someone thinks, but cannot be proven.

I. Read the story. Circle the opinions that are from *Britton Finds a Kitten*.

 a. "Kittens love tuna fish," he thought.

 b. She was white all over, with patches of orange fur.

 c. "It's natural for cats to scratch things."

 d. "Patches is a great pet."

2-3. Write two facts from the story.

_____

- -

_____

_____

- -

_____

_____

- -

_____

Name _____

Vocabulary

Draw a line to match each word on the left with a word or words on the right that have a similar meaning.

mature   details

natural   grown up

features   normal

Now use each word on the left in a sentence of your own.

1. mature _____

_____

_____

2. natural _____

_____

_____

3. features _____

_____

All About the Weather

SUMMARY Today, we have scientific instruments to help us predict the weather. Long ago, however, these instruments had yet to be invented. People, therefore, relied on examining changes in the sky, plants, and animals to predict the weather. This book explores some of the folklore associated with weather prediction.

LESSON VOCABULARY

downpour	harsh
overcast	

INTRODUCE THE BOOK

INTRODUCE THE TITLE AND AUTHOR Before reading the title, view the cover with the group, and ask children to predict what the book might be about. Make sure they identify the clouds and the weather vane, which shows the direction in which the wind blows. Then read the title and author's name with them, and confirm that this book will be about the weather. Further mention that this book will not tell them the way we predict the weather today, but the ways people predicted the weather long ago.

BUILD BACKGROUND Say the word *folklore*, and ask children what they think this word might mean. Some children might equate the word with *folktale*, which is similar. Explain that folklore is what people once believed to explain why different things happened. Mention that people have always been fascinated with the weather and how to predict it. Long ago, people relied on folklore to figure out what the weather would be like.

PREVIEW/TAKE A PICTURE WALK Encourage children to flip through this book, and have them notice features of this nonfiction text. For example, the book has photographs instead of illustrations. Also call attention to the words highlighted in yellow on page 12, and ask children why these words are

highlighted. Explain that these words appear in the book's *glossary;* the glossary tells readers what certain words mean.

ELL Find pictures that can help children understand these four words, *spring, summer, fall,* and *winter,* such as a picture of birds migrating; bears hibernating; a thermometer telling temperature; and a picture that shows all four seasons. Have children point to the corresponding picture and say each word.

READ THE BOOK

SET PURPOSE Invite children to share what they think will be interesting about this book, and encourage them to set a purpose for reading. For example, perhaps children want to learn what frogs have to do with predicting the weather. Instruct children to read closely to find the answers to their questions.

STRATEGY SUPPORT: VISUALIZE Explain that a book usually does not show a picture of every single thing that is told in the story. Readers must sometimes use the words to form pictures in their own imaginations. Remind children that as they read this book, they must use what they know about people and animals, farming, and the weather to picture what is happening.

COMPREHENSION QUESTIONS

PAGE 5 In the poem, what is the sequence of a day? *(morning, then night)*

PAGES 6–7 Look at the clouds on these pages. What is your experience with these kinds of clouds? *(White, puffy clouds mean a nice, sunny day. Very dark clouds mean rain is coming.)*

PAGE 8 How do you know when it might rain? *(Will vary: The air smells damp; the wind picks up; dark clouds come in; the sky gets dark.)*

PAGE 11 What can you tell about the custom of Groundhog Day? *(Many people come to see whether the groundhog sees its shadow.)*

REVIST THE BOOK

THINK AND SHARE

1. Possible response: The author may have wanted to tell that people have been curious about weather for a long time.

2. Possible response: I picture a tree with light green leaves blowing in the wind that comes before a storm.

3. Possible responses: When birds migrate, they travel from place to place to find warm weather.

4. Responses will vary. Accept all responses. Encourage creativity.

EXTEND UNDERSTANDING Invite students to share what they know about modern-day weather prediction. You might show children a weather map from a local paper to jumpstart ideas. Encourage children to compare the ways of predicting the weather today with the ways of predicting weather long ago. Discuss which ways they think are more accurate. Ask: Do you think there is some truth in the old weather folklore? Which do you think is more reliable—weather folklore or modern-day weather prediction? Have children explain their ideas.

RESPONSE OPTIONS

WRITING Invite children to pretend they are weather forecasters today, but instead of using modern terminology, they use folklore to predict the weather. Have children write a weather report using examples of folklore from this book.

SPEAKING AND LISTENING For fun, let children read their weather reports out loud as their classmates listen. Encourage children to identify the folklore that the "weather reporter" has included.

SCIENCE CONNECTION

For one week, invite children to predict the weather, using the folklore in this book. Track how close their predictions are, and discuss the results.

Skill Work

TEACH/REVIEW VOCABULARY

Write the word *downpour* on the board and ask children what it means. Ask for synonyms such as "thunderstorm," "heavy rain," or "raining cats and dogs." Explain that English has many words to describe weather. Next write *overcast* on the board and go through the same exercise. Finally write *harsh* on the board. Ask for antonyms of "harsh weather."

TARGET SKILL AND STRATEGY

AUTHOR'S PURPOSE Speculate with children about the author's purpose for writing this book. For example:

1. Why did the author title this book *All About the Weather? (because this book is a factual book about weather)*

2. Why does the author talk about old weather folklore on page 3, but the photograph shows a weather forecaster today? *(The author is comparing how we predict the weather today with how it was predicted long ago.)*

VISUALIZE Remind children to *visualize*, or picture what they're reading about in their mind, as they read. It's what good readers do. Remind children that if they can picture what is happening as they read, they will better understand and enjoy what they read.

ADDITIONAL SKILL INSTRUCTION

DRAW CONCLUSIONS Explain to children that when we read a book and look at the pictures, we can use what we have read and what we know from real life to figure out more. Tell them that this is called *drawing a conclusion*. Then ask them what kind of conclusions they can draw using what they read as well as what they already know about weather.

Name _____

Author's Purpose

Read the sentences below.

    Sometimes the weather may be rainy. Rain falls from large gray clouds. Rain helps plants grow.

    Sometimes the weather may be sunny. On sunny days, the sun is shining brightly in the sky. Plants need the sun's light to grow.

Why do you think the author wrote these sentences? Use the words in the box to fill in the blanks.

> **rain   weather   grow**

1. The author cares about what plants need to

_____

_____ .

2. The author wants to tell others that plants need

_____

_____ and sun to grow.

3. The author wants to explain that

_____

_____ is important to plants.

Name _____

Vocabulary

Use the correct word from the box to complete each sentence below.

Words to Know
downpour   harsh   overcast

_____

1. A sudden _____
   watered all the flowers and yards on our block.

2. The sun went behind clouds, and the sky grew

   _____

   _____.

   _____

3. When the weather is _____,
   there may be rainstorms or hurricanes or blizzards.

4-5. Write your own sentences using *downpour* and *harsh*.

_____

_____

_____

_____

_____

Learn About Butterflies

SUMMARY This informational text describes the different stages and sequence of the butterfly life cycle. It also includes information about how a butterfly explores its world and how it stays safe from predators.

LESSON VOCABULARY

cycle   develop

insect

INTRODUCE THE BOOK

INTRODUCE THE TITLE AND AUTHOR Discuss with children the title and author of *Learn About Butterflies*. Point out to the children that this is a non-fiction book and ask what information they think might be included in the book.

BUILD BACKGROUND Engage the children in a discussion about butterflies. Invite them to describe butterflies they have seen and share what they know about these interesting insects. Ask: Where have you seen a butterfly? What did it look like? Do you know what and how a butterfly eats? What else do you know about butterflies?

PREVIEW/TAKE A PICTURE WALK Have the children preview the book by looking at the pictures to make predictions about the text. Also call their attention to the labels and captions and explain that these features help them better understand the information in the text. Ask: Based on the photographs, labels, and captions, what do you think you might learn from this book?

READ THE BOOK

SET PURPOSE Based on your initial discussion of butterflies and your preview of the book, ask the children what they are most interested in learning about butterflies. Ask: Is there something you don't know about butterflies that you would like to learn? How do you think this book might help you learn more?

STRATEGY SUPPORT: TEXT STRUCTURE As children read, remind them that certain words help organize and sequence the text. Have the children help you think of examples of these words, such as *first, next, then,* and *last*. Then ask children to find as many signal words as they can in the book. On their own papers, have the children record these words as well as the page numbers where they found them.

COMPREHENSION QUESTIONS

PAGES 4–6 Name and describe the stages of the butterfly life cycle. What does this tell us about butterflies? *(egg, caterpillar, chrysalis/ pupa, butterfly; butterflies go through many changes during their lives)*

PAGE 9 Why do you think a butterfly rests during the night and on rainy days? *(Possible responses: too dark, dangerous, might get wet)*

PAGE 10 How does this butterfly's camouflage make it hard to see? *(It is reddish-brown, just like the leaves.)*

PAGE 12 Why would birds or other insects avoid a brightly colored butterfly? *(because they are poisonous or taste bad)*

PAGE 13 Why do the butterflies come back to the flowers? *(to eat, lay eggs, begin cycle again)*

REVISIT THE BOOK

THINK AND SHARE

1. Opinion: The colors make the butterfly beautiful. It is an opinion because it cannot be proven that a butterfly is beautiful. Fact: Butterflies use their camouflage colors to hide. We can observe butterflies in their habitat or read about them in a book to prove this. Personal opinions will vary.
2. First: color is camouflage; next: color signals bad taste, poison, or danger; last: fly away fast
3. there's/there is, caterpillar's/caterpillar is, what's/what is, they're/they are, don't/do not, aren't/are not
4. Answers will vary but should be supported with information from the text.

EXTEND UNDERSTANDING Have children find the highlighted vocabulary words in the text. Ask them to write down what they think these words mean based on their knowledge of the book and the sentences in which they appear. Have children refer to the glossary to check their definitions and aid comprehension. They can add to or change their definitions based on this information before returning to the text.

RESPONSE OPTIONS

WRITING Ask children to write a short description of a butterfly. They should use information they have learned from the book and also include some of the vocabulary words.

SCIENCE CONNECTION

TIME FOR Science

Encourage children to learn more about the butterfly life cycle using the library or the Internet. They can create and illustrate their own diagrams of the butterfly life cycle and write short descriptions of each stage.

Skill Work

TEACH/REVIEW VOCABULARY

Divide the children into pairs or groups and assign one or two words to each group. Ask them to use the glossary to find the definitions and then share the definitions with the others. For greater understanding, help children write a sentence for each word.

TARGET SKILL AND STRATEGY

FACT AND OPINION Remind children that *facts* are pieces of information that can be proved to be true and *opinions* are pieces of information that people think, but cannot be proven to be true. Facts help readers understand important information about characters, plot, and setting. Opinions are ideas readers can form about a book, character, or situation based on information they have read.

TEXT STRUCTURE Provide children with a graphic organizer to track the stages of the butterfly life cycle as they read. Include signal words such as *first, next, then,* and *last* to help them organize and sequence the information. Ask them to write a short description of each stage.

ADDITIONAL SKILL INSTRUCTION

CAUSE AND EFFECT Call children's attention to page 6 and assist them in identifying what has happened and why. Say: "The butterfly pushes out of the chrysalis because the pupa has finished developing into a butterfly. After that, something else happens. Why does the butterfly shiver, and what does it do next?" *(Because its wings are wet; sits in the sun to dry)*

ELL English language learners may benefit from working with a partner. They can dictate the information to their partners and then practice their skills by reading back the written sentences.

Name _____

Fact and Opinion

Read each question below. Then write the answer using facts or opinions from the book.

1. What insect is this book about?

_____

- -

_____

2. What stage of a butterfly's life cycle comes just before it becomes a butterfly?

_____

- -

_____

3. What does a butterfly's feet help it do?

_____

- -

_____

4. On page 10, what does the author feel that colors do to a butterfly?

_____

- -

_____

- -

_____

5. Why are the wings of a butterfly important?

_____

- -

_____

- -

_____

Name _____

Vocabulary

Use the words in the box to help you complete each sentence.

Words to Know
cycle   develop   insect

1. A butterfly is a type of _____ .

2. The butterfly life _____ begins with an egg.

3. The caterpillar will _____ into a butterfly inside the chrysalis.

4-5. Write two sentences about facts you learned from *Butterflies*. Use the three words from the box in your sentences.

_____

_____

_____

_____

Monarchs Migrate South

SUMMARY Every year, Monarch butterflies leave their summer homes in the north and fly south, where they all live together to stay warm. When spring comes, they fly north, all the way back to where they started. There they lay eggs that will hatch into new Monarchs that will migrate south again. This narrative nonfiction book tells the story of this colorful migration.

LESSON VOCABULARY

hibernate	insects
migrate	nectar
survive	temperature

INTRODUCE THE BOOK

INTRODUCE THE TITLE AND AUTHOR Before reading the title, view the cover with the group and ask children to predict what the book might be about. Make sure they identify butterflies; guide discussion to name Monarch butterflies. Then read the title and the author's name with children, and confirm that this book will be about Monarch butterflies that migrate.

BUILD BACKGROUND Say the word *migrate* and ask if anyone knows what it means. Explain that to *migrate* is to move someplace else. Tell children that some animals migrate to escape cold weather. Mention that they have probably seen birds migrate when the weather grows cool in the fall. Ask them what they think happens when the weather gets warm again. Remind children that this book will be about butterflies that migrate.

PREVIEW/TAKE A PICTURE WALK Encourage children to look through the book, and have them notice features of the text. For instance, the book has photographs instead of drawings. Also call attention to words that are in dark letters and are highlighted with yellow. Ask children why they think these words are treated differently. Tell them that these words appear in the book's Glossary—a kind of dictionary that appears at the back of a book.

ELL Ask children for the word in their home language that means *butterfly*. Find pictures that can help children understand these words: *migrate, nectar, survive*. Have children point to the corresponding picture(s) and say each word.

READ THE BOOK

SET PURPOSE Invite children to share what they think will be interesting about this book, and encourage them to set a purpose for reading. For instance, perhaps children want to know where Monarchs go when the weather gets cold. Instruct children to read closely to find the answers to their questions.

STRATEGY SUPPORT: PRIOR KNOWLEDGE Remind children that *prior knowledge* is the information that they already know about a topic. Tell them to think about what they already know about butterflies, Monarch butterflies, and migration as they read the book.

COMPREHENSION QUESTIONS

PAGE 3 What makes it difficult for Monarch butterflies to survive? *(long, cold winters)*

PAGE 4 Which Monarch butterflies make the long migration? *(those born in the late summer and early fall)*

PAGE 5 What is the first thing Monarchs must do to get ready for their migration? *(eat a lot of food so they can store fat)*

PAGES 7–8 Where do Monarchs migrate and how do they know where to go? *(They fly south; they just know where to go.)*

PAGE 12 What do Monarchs do during the winter? *(hang in trees, stay together for safety, get ready to fly north)*

REVISIT THE BOOK

THINK AND SHARE

1. It will eat a lot and store fat for its long trip. They need the food to make the long trip south.

2. Responses will vary; prompt the words *insects* and *nectar* as children share their prior knowledge.

3. *warm, cool, short, long, big, high, low, safe*

4. Responses will vary but should include that the author wanted to teach children about Monarch butterflies.

EXTEND UNDERSTANDING Invite students to share what they know about butterflies and migration. You might bring a calendar and explain that cooler weather in the North prompts Monarchs to migrate. Talk about the months in which the weather grows cool. Use the calendar to predict in which months the weather is too cold for Monarch butterflies in the North. Then use the calendar to predict when migrating Monarchs and birds are likely to return to the North.

RESPONSE OPTIONS

WRITING Have children write about their favorite or least favorite time of year. If they were to migrate, when it would be and why? Encourage children to use such words as *survive* and *temperature*.

SPEAKING AND LISTENING Let children read what they have written while their classmates listen.

SCIENCE CONNECTION

TIME FOR **Science**

Ask children if they know of other animals that migrate. Discuss birds that fly south in the cold weather and return north in warmer weather. Tell them that "flyways" exist for birds to rest in during their long yearly migrations. Consider bringing in a DVD of "Winged Migration," the award-winning documentary about birds that migrate long distances.

Skill Work

TEACH/REVIEW VOCABULARY

Write the words *survive, temperature, hibernate,* and *migrate* on the board and have children explain what each word means. Then, after saying each word, talk about how all the words relate to surviving.

TARGET SKILL AND STRATEGY

DRAW CONCLUSIONS Tell students that readers draw conclusions about what they're reading based on clues the writer gives them. Say: The writer of *Monarchs Migrate South* told us that Monarch butterflies migrate south during the winter. They stay together to keep warm. In the spring, they return to their homes in the North. Based on these clues, what conclusion can you draw about Monarch butterflies? *(They like being warm; they migrate in order to stay warm.)*

PRIOR KNOWLEDGE Remind children that *prior knowledge* refers to what they already know about the topic. Model: When fall comes, the weather grows cooler, and the days grow shorter. This may prompt Monarch butterflies to migrate. If they are to survive, the butterflies must fly south to warmer weather, like some birds. When spring comes, the weather grows warmer, and the days grow longer. This is when migrating butterflies and birds fly north for the summer.

ADDITIONAL SKILL INSTRUCTION

AUTHOR'S PURPOSE Speculate with children about the author's purpose for writing this book. For example:

1. Why did the author call this book *Monarchs Migrate South*? *(It tells exactly what the book is about.)*

2. Why do you think the author wrote about Monarchs instead of some other kind of butterfly? *(Monarchs take the longest trip of any butterfly; they are very interesting.)*

Name _____

Draw Conclusions

Read the story below.

> Monarch butterflies start as eggs, grow into caterpillars, and then change into butterflies. Every winter, after they have become butterflies, Monarchs migrate south. They must eat a lot of food for their trip south. During their trip, Monarchs rest each night. Once they arrive in the south, many Monarchs hang on trees together. When spring comes, Monarchs fly back north and lay their eggs.

Based on what you have read, what do you think will happen next? Write your ideas below.

_____
_____
_____
_____
_____
_____
_____
_____
_____
_____
_____

Name _____

Vocabulary

Use the correct words from the box to complete each sentence.

Words to Know

hibernate	insect	migrate
nectar	survive	temperature

1. Monarch butterflies _____ to Mexico,

   where the winter _____ is much warmer.

2. A butterfly is an _____ that eats

   _____ from flowers.

3. Some animals _____, or sleep deeply,

   in order to _____ cold weather.

4. Write a sentence of your own using two words from the box.

   _____

   _____

   _____

Cascarones Are for Fun

SUMMARY Cascarones are introduced to readers in this informative and useful book. Children will read about the history of cascarones, why they are pretty, and how they are made.

LESSON VOCABULARY

celebrate	cherish	China
confetti	decorate	empress
Italy	Mexico	perfume

INTRODUCE THE BOOK

INTRODUCE THE TITLE AND AUTHOR Discuss with the children the title and the author of *Cascarones Are for Fun*. Based on the title and the cover illustration, ask the children what they think they will discover in this book. Talk about anything in the cover picture that looks familiar to the children.

BUILD BACKGROUND Point to China, Italy, and Mexico on a map. Tell the children they will be reading about a cherished custom that is similar in these far apart countries.

Ask if anyone knows what cascarones are. If anyone does, ask him or her to tell why they are fun. For the children who do not know, talk about cascarones and what the people on the cover are doing. If children know of other customs involving eggs, encourage them to describe them to the class.

PREVIEW/TAKE A PICTURE WALK As the children look through the illustrations and headings in the book, ask them to predict what the people are making and explain whether it looks like fun. Ask if anyone knows what country the flag on page 13 represents.

READ THE BOOK

SET PURPOSE Encourage the children to think about finding out about cascarones and set their own purpose for reading this book. If they have been given some background on how cascarones are part of Mexican celebrations, they will have more chance to decide on their own reason for reading.

STRATEGY SUPPORT: MONITOR AND FIX UP This reader covers not only how to make cascarones, but also their purpose, how they arose in history, and the countries using cascarones. The children may need to reread and review the material so that they can keep straight the facts and steps. Monitoring skills like reread and review will also help students to be able to draw conclusions about why cascarones are important in celebrations.

COMPREHENSION QUESTIONS

PAGE 5 How are cascarones used in Mexico? *(They are cracked over your head to bring luck.)*

PAGE 6 What happens to the raw egg when preparing cascarones? *(It is blown out of the shell.)*

PAGE 7 What is confetti? *(tiny pieces of colored paper)*

PAGE 9 Where did Marco Polo find cascarones? *(China)*

PAGE 10 Why did young men in Italy toss cascarones to young women? *(Young men liked to show affection toward young women that way.)*

REVIVIT THE BOOK

THINK AND SHARE
1. Responses will vary.
2. Responses will vary but should include that readers should look at the pictures and reread anything they don't understand.
3. Responses will vary.
4. Possible response: p. 6: Small holes are made in both ends of an egg. The raw egg is blown out from inside the shell and the egg is later decorated and then filled; p. 9: Marco Polo brought cascarones to Italy from China; p. 12: Cascarones are now used in Mexico and parts of the United States to celebrate Carnival and the Fifth of May.

EXTEND UNDERSTANDING Because there are many facts contained in this reader, children can draw conclusions after reading each section. Help children to do so with each section and then ask them to make one conclusion about the whole book. Remind them to go back and look at the title of the book and the headings when they make this broad statement.

RESPONSE OPTIONS
WRITING Some children may be interested in making a cookbook about leftover eggs, as described on pages 14-15. Others may like to make a "Fun Book of Party Activities." Children may first have to interview one another to find out favorite games and crafts. Remind them to make pictures to accompany any activities involving steps.

SOCIAL STUDIES CONNECTION

Time For SOCIAL STUDIES

Encourage children to make a map showing all the places where people celebrated with cascarones. Have them make a route between the countries and write a sentence explaining how cascarones might have spread.

Skill Work

TEACH/REVIEW VOCABULARY
Group the words, *celebrate, confetti, decorate,* and *perfume* together and ask children to guess why all these words are used in a book about a celebration custom. Help children to see that certain words often go together—especially when we are talking about activities we all care about such as parties and family celebrations.

ELL Ask volunteers to identify anything like cascarones in events and celebrations they have in their home countries. Have them describe these items—their color, composition, uses, and so on.

TARGET SKILL AND STRATEGY
DRAW CONCLUSIONS Ask: What conclusion can you draw from the picture on page 5? Is the girl being mean or funny? Then ask: Why do you think Empress Carlotta changed the cascarone's contents from perfume to confetti? Encourage children to think logically and use their own experiences, reread if necessary, and look at the illustrations to draw their conclusions.

MONITOR AND FIX UP In order to draw valid conclusions, children need to understand what they read. Sometimes the best way to do this is to reread and review. If some children do not understand how the cascarones came to Mexico, ask them to reread page 11 and look at the map. Ask where they think Empress Carlotta came from. (You may need to point out the route show on the map from Italy to Mexico.)

ADDITIONAL SKILL INSTRUCTION
REALISM AND FANTASY Have children review pages 6–8. Point out that as with any set of instructions, the order of the steps involved in making cascarones is important. Call attention to the sequence clue words such as *first, then,* and *afterward.* Suggest that children find other clue words that help them understand the order of the steps in making cascarones.

Name _____

Draw Conclusions

Think about these questions.
Draw a line to the conclusion that best answers the question.

1. Should you worry when the egg is cracked over your head?

2. Why do you celebrate special days with cascarones?

3. How can you get confetti into cascarones?

4. What happens to a good idea like the one Marco Polo found in China?

5. Why have cascarones on the Fifth of May?

The egg is first blown out.

It is easy to spread fun things.

Cascarones are made of eggshells.

Cascarones are fun and bring good luck.

Cascarones are made for celebrations.

Name _____

Vocabulary

Read the two choices after each sentence. Choose the best word from the word box to complete each sentence. Circle it.

Words to Know
celebrate   cherish   China   confetti decorate   empress   Italy   Mexico   perfume

1. People use cascarones to _____.   cook   celebrate

2. Cascarones started long ago in _____.   China   Mexico

3. Long ago, they were filled with _____.   confetti   perfume

4. The Empress brought cascarones to _____.   Italy   Mexico

5. People _____ the cascarones custom.   dance   cherish

6. Today cascarones are filled with _____.   candy   confetti

7. People like to _____ cascarones.   decorate   cook

8. Marco Polo came from _____.   Italy   Mexico

9. The _____ put confetti inside.   empress   Marco Polo

Jamie's Jumble of Junk

SUMMARY Children read about a boy who finds a creative use for some junk he has been saving.

LESSON VOCABULARY

carve	fabulous
imagination	original
peer	royal
sighed	tangle

INTRODUCE THE BOOK

INTRODUCE THE TITLE AND AUTHOR Discuss the title and author of *Jamie's Jumble of Junk*. Then ask children to tell what they think this book might be about and discuss what kind of junk Jamie might have. Talk about what the word jumble might mean. Guide children to understand that a jumble is a pile of many different things all mixed up together.

BUILD BACKGROUND Discuss recycling with children. Invite them to share any experiences they have had using recycled objects for a new purpose. Ask: Did you ever save junk because you thought you would use it again? Did you use it in a new way?

PREVIEW/TAKE A PICTURE WALK Invite children to take a picture walk to preview the text and illustrations. Discuss what kinds of junk Jamie keeps in his room and what he might use it for. Ask children what they hope to find out as they read the story. Record their comments.

READ THE BOOK

SET PURPOSE Have children set a purpose for reading *Jamie's Jumble of Junk*. Ask them to think about what kind of project they might make for a school fair to show what they are learning. Have them also read to find some of the answers to the questions they raised as they previewed the book.

STRATEGY SUPPORT: VISUALIZE Tell children that paying attention to the details the writer uses as well as details in the illustrations will help them form pictures in their minds. Model how to visualize what Jamie does on page 4: I read that Jamie carefully saved paper, ribbons, and boxes. I can almost see the shiny, curly ribbons. I can feel the crisp colorful paper in my hands and hear it crinkle as I fold it neatly. Visualizing these details helps me understand how Jamie might feel as he saves these things.

COMPREHENSION QUESTIONS

PAGE 3 Why does Jamie's mother want him to get rid of some junk? *(She says there won't be any room for him.)* Why does she shake her head when he says he has plenty of room? *(She doesn't understand why he wants all the stuff in his room.)*

PAGE 7 How did Jamie probably get the idea for his project? *(Possible response: Looking at his junk gave him the idea.)*

PAGE 13 The principal said that Jamie's project was important for two reasons. What were the reasons? *(The project was about people and it was about recycling.)*

REVISIT THE BOOK

THINK AND SHARE

1. Responses may vary, but should include a plausible theme and details that support the theme. Possible response: Lesson: Don't let what other people think keep you from doing what you think is important.
Details: Jamie's friends don't understand his junk; Mother shakes her head at Jamie; a boy says Jamie's project is a bunch of junk.

2. Responses will vary but should reflect children's ability to visualize details such as yarn hair and blue paper clothing covering a body made of cardboard boxes.

3. Possible response: Imagination is using your mind to come up with a brand-new idea.

4. Possible response: People recycle because many things we use once can be used again in a new way. It is wasteful to use something one time and throw it away. Children can recycle by not throwing out bottles and cans. They can use both sides of every piece of paper.

EXTEND UNDERSTANDING Explain to children that recycling centers sort used objects into groups, depending on materials in them. Groups of materials that are commonly recycled include metal, glass, plastic and paper. Have children brainstorm items from home or school that could be recycled or reused in a new way.

RESPONSE OPTIONS

SPEAKING Have children work with partners to prepare a public service announcement about recycling. They can practice together and then present their announcement to the class.

ART CONNECTION

Provide a wide range of found and recyclable objects such as buttons, jar lids, cardboard tubes, egg cartons, and tin foil. Challenge children to create an object from the materials that fits a theme or topic they are learning about in science or social studies. Ask children to present their finished creations.

Skill Work

TEACH/REVIEW VOCABULARY

Turn to page 9 and read the sentence: "I AM using my imagination!" Jamie said proudly." Ask children if the author could have used a different word in place of *imagination*. List any suggestions. Reread the sentence with children's offerings. Ask: Does the sentence still mean the same thing? Repeat with *fabulous* (page 4) and *peered* (page 7). Then ask children to make up new sentences with the vocabulary words.

ELL Write each of the following expressions from the story on large sentence strips: "It's OK." "I'll think of something." "I don't know." "I've got an idea." "What are you doing?" "Yippeee!" Say each expression using gestures and facial expressions and have children repeat it after you. Discuss when the expressions might be used appropriately.

TARGET SKILL AND STRATEGY

THEME Remind children that a *theme* is the big idea or lesson of a story. Briefly discuss the theme of some stories children have read recently. Call particular attention to any fables they have read. Discuss what the author of *Jamie's Jumble of Junk* wants readers to understand about using imagination and reusing old things.

VISUALIZE Remind children that they can use different senses to fully imagine, understand, and enjoy their reading. Reread page 3 from *Jamie's Jumble of Junk* and have children describe the images they picture.

ADDITIONAL SKILL INSTRUCTION

DRAW CONCLUSIONS Remind children that when they draw conclusions, they put together details from the text and pictures with what they already know to figure out something new. Direct children's attention to the text on page 9 and ask children why Jamie thought his mother would be glad. Guide them to recall that Jamie's mother had wanted him to get rid of the junk earlier in the story. Ask what experiences they have had that helped them draw this conclusion.

Name _____

Theme

The **theme** is the lesson or big idea a story teaches.
Fill in the boxes below to find the theme of *Jamie's Jumble of Junk*.

Beginning: _____
_____
_____
_____

↓

Middle: _____
_____
_____
_____

↓

End: _____
_____
_____
_____

What Jamie learns: _____
_____
_____
_____
_____

Name _____

Vocabulary

Answer the questions about the vocabulary words.

Words to Know			
carve	fabulous	imagination	original
peer	royal	sighed	tangle

1. Name something that is **royal** blue. _____

_____

2. Name something you can **carve**. _____

_____

3. Name something that can **tangle**. _____

_____

4. Name something you can **peer** through. _____

5. Tell about something you do with your **imagination**.

_____

_____

6. Tell about something that is **original**.

_____

_____

7. Tell about something you did that was **fabulous**.

_____

_____

8. Tell about a time you **sighed**.

_____

_____

America's Home

SUMMARY The White House has been a symbol of our nation for more than 200 years. The first President to live there was John Adams, our second President. This nonfiction book gives information about the history, roles, and accessibility of the official home of American Presidents.

LESSON VOCABULARY

law	nation
President	soldiers
symbol	tourist
vote	

INTRODUCE THE BOOK

INTRODUCE THE TITLE AND AUTHOR Discuss with children the title and author of *America's Home*. Have children share their reactions to the photograph on the cover. Point out the *Social Studies* label and ask: How might this be a Social Studies book? Remind them that Social Studies includes history.

BUILD BACKGROUND Discuss what children know about the White House. Ask: Who lives in the White House? Where is the White House located? Why does a country need an official home for its leader? Do you know anyone who has visited the White House?

PREVIEW/TAKE A PICTURE WALK Invite children to turn the pages of the book and preview the photographs and captions. Turn to pages 4–5. Read the captions and names. Ask: Have you heard about these Presidents before? What do they all have in common? (*All were elected President; all lived in the White House.*) Ask children why they think this book has photographs instead of illustrations. (*It is a nonfiction book about a real place, and photographs exist that show the White House and its residents.*) Ask children to name the President who lives in the White House now.

READ THE BOOK

SET PURPOSE Have children set a purpose for reading *America's Home*. Curiosity voiced about the topic or questions generated while previewing the book can guide this purpose. Suggest that, while children read, they think about homes where elected leaders such as the President or their governor live and how those places are different from other people's homes.

STRATEGY SUPPORT: IMPORTANT IDEAS Remind children that they will read about many ideas, and that some ideas are more important than others. *Important ideas* tell more about the main idea of the text. Encourage children to look for important ideas as they read *America's Home*.

COMPREHENSION QUESTIONS

PAGES 3 AND 6 How are the houses in these two pictures the same? How are they different? (*Both buildings are white and two stories tall; page 3 shows a pointed porch while page 6 shows a rounded one; there is a flag above the White House on page 3 and a big lantern above the front door; there is a little evergreen on the lawn of page 6.*)

PAGE 7 Why was it important to save the picture of George Washington? (*He was our country's first President.*)

PAGES 7–8 Who burned the White House? (*soldiers from England in the War of 1812*)

PAGE 11 Who are the children pictured on page 11? (*They are children who lived in the White House when their father, Theodore Roosevelt, was President.*)

PAGE 13 How much does it cost to visit the White House? (*It is free.*)

REVIST THE BOOK

THINK AND SHARE

1. Responses will vary, but information from the book should be stated.
2. Possible response: I learned that the families of presidents live at the White House. It helped me understand why the White House has a movie theatre and a swimming pool.
3. Symbol: an object that stands for something else; nation: a group of people living in one country; tourist: someone traveling for enjoyment. Sentences should use each word correctly.
4. Responses will vary but should mention information linked to the book.

EXTEND UNDERSTANDING As children look at the photographs, ask them what other important buildings they know about. Point out that the governor of each state has an official residence, and that many Presidents' birthplaces are also open to the public. Ask: When does a President have to move from the White House? *(when the newly elected President is ready to move in)*

RESPONSE OPTIONS

WRITING Ask children to imagine that they have a friend who has never heard of the White House. Have them write a few sentences explaining what the White House is and why it is important. Encourage children to draw pictures and use captions to go with their explanations.

SOCIAL STUDIES CONNECTION

Have children write and illustrate one or two details of their own house and compare it with the White House. Direct their attention to page 10 for details they might use to compare the two residences.

Time For **SOCIAL STUDIES**

Skill Work

TEACH/REVIEW VOCABULARY

Write *President* on the board. Ask children for the definition, and then ask them to name the current President of the United States. Write *symbol, vote,* and *nation* on the board and define each one, using the Glossary on page 16 of *America's Home.* Then use each word in a sentence.

ELL Print each vocabulary word on a card. Place the cards face down in a pile. Have children take turns picking a card and making up a riddle to help others guess the word. For example, "This word is the name of the top leader of our country."

TARGET SKILL AND STRATEGY

DETAILS AND FACTS Tell children that *details and facts* support the main idea of a book. The main idea of this book is that the White House is America's official, important "home." Details and facts from the story help explain this idea. Ask children to find three details or facts about the White House and read them aloud.

IMPORTANT IDEAS Ask: What important ideas did you read about in *America's Home*? How do you know they are important? Have children create a web and write *The White House* in the middle. Have them add important ideas to the outer circles.

ADDITIONAL SKILL INSTRUCTION

CAUSE AND EFFECT As they read, children should think about what happens and why. Offer an example: Because it was raining, I got wet. Ask children to identify what happened (*I got wet*) and why it happened (*it was raining*). Point out that clue words such as *because* help readers figure out cause and effect. Ask children to identify what happened to the White House in 1812—(*soldiers burned it*) and why it happened (*they were at war with the United States*).

Name _____

Details and Facts

Think about **details** and **facts** you have learned about the White House. Read each question below. Then circle the best answer. Look back at the book if you need to.

1. Where is the White House located?

   a. New York City   **b.** San Francisco   **c.** Washington, D.C.

2. How many rooms are in the White House today?

   a. more than 130   **b.** fewer than 100   **c.** no one knows

3. Which of these features is NOT part of the White House?

   a. a movie theater   **b.** a complete zoo   **c.** a jogging track

4. Soldiers from which country burned the White House in 1812?

   a. England   **b.** France   **c.** Spain

5. Who lives in the White House?

   a. the Vice-President of the United States   **b.** the President of the United States   **c.** visitors to the United States

Name _____

Vocabulary

Words to Know

law	nation	President	soldiers
symbol	tourist	vote	

Pick a word or words from the box to finish each sentence.

1. Citizens _____ to elect a President every four years.

2. The White House is an important _____ of

   our _____.

3. It is possible for a _____ to take a free tour of the White House.

4. The _____ makes sure that every

   _____ of our country is obeyed.

5. The White House was burned by enemy

   _____ in 1812.

95

Go West!

SUMMARY Children read about Sara's family, who moves west to Montana in search of a better life. At first, Sara does not want to leave her friends or her favorite books and toys. Later, when a rainstorm turns the trail to mud, Sara experiences the hardest day of her life, and gains a new outlook on her new life.

LESSON VOCABULARY

errand	familiar
favorite	impression
memory	stampede

INTRODUCE THE BOOK

INTRODUCE THE TITLE AND AUTHOR Discuss the title and author of *Go West!* Based on the title and the illustration on the cover, ask children to describe what they think this book might be about. Ask children if they think the story takes place today or long ago and how they know.

BUILD BACKGROUND Explain that long ago, many people in the Untied States traveled west to find new homes and a better life. Many traveled west in wagon trains. The trip was long, dangerous, and difficult. The covered wagons, pulled by animals, were small and crowded. Families had to leave behind most of their belongings. Ask children what they might have taken along if they traveled by wagon train to a new home.

PREVIEW/TAKE A PICTURE WALK Invite children to take a picture walk to preview the text and illustrations. Ask them how the scenes of long ago seem similar to or different from life today.

READ THE BOOK

SET PURPOSE Have children set a purpose for reading *Go West!* For example, they might read to find out what it is like to travel on a wagon train. Encourage children to keep their purpose in mind as they read.

STRATEGY SUPPORT: QUESTIONING Tell children that readers learn more if they ask themselves questions as they read. They can stop and think about parts of a story they do not understand, as well asking themselves what they want to know. Asking questions helps them look for answers as they keep reading. Model: As I read the top of page 4, I wonder why Sara wouldn't want to leave her cramped, noisy home. As I keep reading, I see the things she likes about this place. Now I understand why she doesn't want to leave.

COMPREHENSION QUESTIONS

PAGE 3–4 Why does Sara try not to listen when Papa talks about moving away from the city for a better life? (*She does not want to leave the only home she knows.*)

PAGES 6–7 Why must Sara's family leave most of their belongings behind? (*They are going far away; most likely it would be hard to carry many of their belongings with them.*)

PAGE 15 Why does Sara probably decide that everything would be okay? (*She has already had to do something really hard and she succeeded.*)

REVISIT THE BOOK

THINK AND SHARE

1. Responses will vary. Possible responses given: *Facts:* People moved from cities to Montana for new homes and more space. People had to leave many belongings behind when they moved. It was hard to drive the wagons across the fields. *Details:* Montana had plenty of land. Sara's family left their dishes and piano in the city. The mules did not stay on the trail. The trail was rocky ad muddy in the rain.
2. Responses will vary. Possible response: I wanted to know what it was like to go in a wagon train. I found out it was crowded and bumpy.
3. Response will vary. Possible context clues: *struggled*: hard to drive; *belongings*: dishes, piano, pie plate, fiddle, doll; *impression*: know what Montana would be like; *vast*: mountains to climb and rivers to cross.
4. Responses will vary. Possible response: I would take the blocks that used to be my dad's and my favorite book.

EXTEND UNDERSTANDING Explain that writers often write stories that tell about events that happened long ago. The characters are made up, but the story details tell about things that could have happened to real people. Discuss story events that could only have taken place in the past and other events that could happen today.

RESPONSE OPTIONS

WORD WORK Write the compound words *someday, upstairs, notebook, everything,* and *goodbye* with individual word parts on separate index cards. Have children work with partner to match up the word parts and talk about the word meaning.

SOCIAL STUDIES CONNECTION

Time For SOCIAL STUDIES

Display a map of the United States. Help children find Montana. Explain that some Eastern cities were very crowded about 100 to 150 years ago. The government allowed people to come to Montana and work to buy land. The railroads offered reduced-price tickets for pioneers to travel by train to Montana. Have children roleplay discussions in which they discuss whether to move to Montana or stay in crowded cities.

ELL Show children illustrations or photos of Conestoga wagons, mules, and related words from the selection such as *fiddle, wagon, train, piano,* and *tools.* Also provide labels for each picture. After introducing the words and pictures, mix up the labels and have children match them up and name the corresponding pictures.

Skill Work

TEACH/REVIEW VOCABULARY

Have children respond to the following questions to build understanding of the story vocabulary: What *errand* do you do on the weekend? Are the people in your neighborhood *familiar*? What is your *favorite memory*? What *impression* did you have about school at the beginning of the year? What are some things that could *stampede*?

TARGET SKILL AND STRATEGY

FACTS AND DETAILS Tell children that facts are bits of information that can be proven to be true. Details are bits of information that tell more about important ideas in a story. Both the text and the illustrations may give details. Ask: What details help you understand how Sara felt as she drove the wagon?

QUESTIONING Remind children to pause to ask themselves questions as they read. Suggest that they make a quick picture or comment on a sticky note and attach it the part of the text they are questioning. Then they can return to it after they read and decide whether the reading answered their question.

ADDITIONAL SKILL INSTRUCTION

COMPARE AND CONTRAST Remind children that thinking about how things are alike or different gives readers a better understand of the two things they are comparing. Have children discuss how Sara's new home on the wagon train is like her old home. How is it different?

Name _____

Facts and Details

Thinking about **facts** and **details** can help you better understand what you read.

Read each event from the story. Circle the detail that helps you understand it.

1. Sara did not want to leave the city.

   Her friend lived upstairs and her teacher was nice.

   Her parents came home late from the factories.

2. The family would leave most of their things behind.

   Gerda promised she would write letters.

   They left their dishes and the piano.

3. It was hard to sleep on the train.

   Mr. Howe took Sara's family to the train station.

   The train was noisy and the seats were hard.

4. The rain made it hard to drive the wagon.

   Papa guided the mules and Sara held the reins.

   Mama sat in the back with Agnes.

5. What detail shows that Sara thought things would be okay in Montana?

   _____

   -

   _____

   _____

   -

Name _____

Vocabulary

Draw a line from each word to its meaning.

1. errand   something you remember

2. familiar   a quick trip to do a job

3. favorite   an idea or feeling

4. impression   a rush of wild animals

5. memory   best-liked

6. stampede   something well known

Write a sentence using two vocabulary words from the list above.

_____

- -

_____

- -

_____

Double Trouble Twins

SUMMARY Peter and Sam were twins who were always getting into trouble. So much trouble that their mother called them Double Trouble. One day while playing with a skateboard, they broke their mother's vase. They both decided to earn money to repair the vase. They baby-sat for their neighbors, and their mother forgave them for breaking the vase.

LESSON VOCABULARY

jealous   relatives
sibling

INTRODUCE THE BOOK

INTRODUCE THE TITLE AND AUTHOR Discuss with children the title and the author of *Double Trouble Twins*. Ask children to think about the title and look at the illustration on the cover. Ask: What do you think the story will be about?

BUILD BACKGROUND Ask children if any of them know twins. If any twins are in the class, ask what they like and dislike about being twins. Ask the other children what they think they would like and dislike about being a twin.

PREVIEW/TAKE A PICTURE WALK Ask children to take a picture walk and look at all of the illustrations in the book. Ask: Do the illustrations seem to tell a story? What do you think the story will be about now?

READ THE BOOK

SET PURPOSE Have children set a purpose for reading *Double Trouble Twins*. Student's curiosity about twins may guide this purpose. Talk about what questions the children may have about twins before they set a purpose for reading.

STRATEGY SUPPORT: STORY STRUCTURE Remind children that every story has a beginning, middle, and end. Each event in a story leads to the next event. When they think about how all these events fit together, they can tell what the story is all about. Have children summarize the events that make up the beginning of *Double Trouble Twins*.

COMPREHENSION QUESTIONS

PAGE 5 What kind of pancakes did the twins love to eat? *(blueberry)*

PAGE 7 What did the twins do one Thanksgiving? *(They knocked the turkey off the plate.)*

PAGE 8 What was the twins' father doing when they broke the vase? *(He was in the basement fixing Peter's table.)*

PAGE 11 What does the neighbor suggest that Sam and Peter do when they ask him for work? *(She suggests they babysit her five-year-old twins.)*

PAGES 12–13 What do you think Peter and Sam learned from babysitting the twins? *(Possible response: That twins really are double trouble.)*

PAGE 15 What does Sam and Peter's mother do when she finds out they broke her vase? *(She forgives them.)*

REVISIT THE BOOK

THINK AND SHARE

1. Possible response: You should take responsibility for your actions.
2. Beginning: Peter and Sam break their mother's vase. Middle: The boys watch Tim and Tina to earn money to fix the vase.
End: The boys understand they were both at fault. They tell their mother they both broke the vase.
3. Possible responses: break/fast, blue/berry, skate/board, after/noon, any/one
4. Possible responses: Like: always have someone to play with, people treat you special. Dislike: hard to feel special just for myself, people always lump us together.

EXTEND UNDERSTANDING Have the children summarize the story in their own words. Help them to understand that the story, or plot, has a beginning, middle and an end.

RESPONSE OPTIONS

SPEAKING Ask children what they think the twins learned by the end of the story.

SOCIAL STUDIES CONNECTION

Time For SOCIAL STUDIES

Have children write and illustrate a family album of their own family with a description and illustration of a family member on each page.

Skill Work

TEACH/REVIEW VOCABULARY

Review the vocabulary words. Then play Vocabulary Master with children. Give children three different definitions for each vocabulary word, including one that is fantastical or silly, and have them select the correct definition and then use the word in a sentence.

ELL Ask English learners to skim the story and write down any unfamiliar words. Help them by providing them with definitions for each word.

TARGET SKILL AND STRATEGY

THEME Review that the theme of a story is the "big idea" or the lesson that readers learn from the story. Encourage children to consider the theme of this story. Ask: Why do Sam and Peter get into so much trouble? What do they learn by watching Tim and Tina?

STORY STRUCTURE As children read, have them pay attention to the events that happen in the beginning, middle, and end of the story. Call out a few events, and encourage children to tell you if they happened in the beginning, middle, or end of the story. For example, say: During what part of the story do Sam and Peter offer to take care of the twins? *(middle)*

ADDITIONAL SKILL INSTRUCTION

REALISM/FANTASY Remind children that a story that is *realistic* is one that seems just like real life. Remind children that a story that is a *fantasy* is one that seems not like real life, such as a story in which cows talk or children can fly. Based on looking at the illustrations in *The Double Trouble Twins*, have children guess whether this story is realistic or a fantasy.

Name _____

Theme

Read the story below.

> Kim picked up her list of chores for the day. She quickly read the top of the list. First, she had to take Daisy, her dog, on a walk. Then she had to clean up the kitchen.
>
> Since she was in the kitchen, Kim decided to clean it first.
>
> As Kim walked Daisy later that morning, it began to rain. Daisy and Kim were wet and muddy by the time they got home.
>
> Daisy ran into the kitchen. "Oh, no!" Kim said. Daisy was getting everything muddy!
>
> "Kim," said her mom, "did you read all the instructions?"
>
> "Well, no . . ." Kim said. She pulled out the list again and read the last part, "Make sure you walk Daisy before it rains!"

What is the "big idea," or theme, of this story?
Write your ideas below.

_____

- -

_____

_____

- -

_____

_____

- -

_____

_____

- -

Name _____

Vocabulary

Each group of words below are related in some way. Choose a word from the Word Box that best completes each group. Write the answer on the line. You may use a word more than once.

Words to Know
jealous   relatives   sibling

1.   mother

    brother

    _____
    - - - - - - - - - - - - - - -
    _____

3.   brother

    sister

    _____
    - - - - - - - - - - - - - - -
    _____

2.   afraid

    sad

    _____
    - - - - - - - - - - - - - - -
    _____

4.   uncle

    grandmother

    _____
    - - - - - - - - - - - - - - -
    _____

5. Draw a time when you felt jealous.

What Makes Buildings Special?

SUMMARY This nonfiction book discusses some of the special ornaments people put on buildings, such as symbols, gargoyles, and griffins. It gives examples of some decorated buildings in different U.S. cities.

LESSON VOCABULARY

discover   dwell   gargoyle
government   griffin   resident
welcome

INTRODUCE THE BOOK

INTRODUCE THE TITLE AND AUTHOR Ask children to locate the title and author on the cover. Ask children what they think the book is going to be about, based on the title.

BUILD BACKGROUND Explain to children that symbols are shapes or figures that have a greater meaning to the people who use them. Explain that the U.S. flag is a symbol for our country. Ask children what ideas they think of when they see the U.S. flag.

PREVIEW/ILLUSTRATIONS Invite children to take a picture walk through the book. Based on their preview, ask children if they think the book is going to be fiction (a "made-up story") or nonfiction ("based on real things"), and what clues they used to figure this out. Also ask children if they think the book is going to be about buildings in just one place or around the country. What clues did they use to answer that?

READ THE BOOK

SET PURPOSE After children have previewed the book, ask them what questions they have and hope to answer by reading the book. Write the questions on the board to discuss after they read the book.

STRATEGY SUPPORT: PREDICT/CONFIRM PREDICTIONS Predicting helps children set a purpose for reading and make sense of the text. As children make predictions about the book, remind them to give reasons for their predictions. Guide them that when they predict, they should think about other books they have read and their own experiences. Remind them to check to see whether their predictions were correct.

COMPREHENSION QUESTIONS

PAGES 4–8 Write the name of a famous building mentioned in the book and one thing that makes it special. (*Responses will vary. Possible answer: Chrysler Building; has the shapes of cars and car parts on it*)

PAGE 4 Find the cause and the effect in this sentence: If you take a close look at the building, you will discover hidden shapes. (*cause: taking a close look at the building; effect: discovering hidden shapes.*)

PAGE 8 What is a griffin? (*A made-up animal that is part eagle and part lion.*)

PAGES 8–9 What do the captions on these pages tell you about each of the gargoyles? (*where they are*)

REVISIT THE BOOK

THINK AND SHARE

1. To help the rain run off the roof.
2. Possible response: I thought the book would be about famous buildings. I was only partly right, because it was really about how people decorate buildings.
3. Responses will vary. Possible answers: I dwell in a house; I am a resident of my town; I welcome my mom when she gets home.
4. Responses will vary.

EXTEND UNDERSTANDING Ask children to think of a symbol not mentioned in the book. Ask them to write it down as well as what they think it means. Examples include dollar sign, cent sign, a ribbon, and a star.

RESPONSE OPTIONS

WRITING Ask the children to write a sentence identifying their favorite building and explaining why. Give them the model: "My favorite building is _____ because it _____."

SOCIAL STUDIES CONNECTION

Time For SOCIAL STUDIES

Show children pictures of buildings from other parts of the world, for example, traditional architecture such as the Forbidden City in Beijing, China, or the Taj Mahal in India. Help children identify the special things on these buildings.

Skill Work

TEACH/REVIEW VOCABULARY

Invite children to read the Glossary at the back of the book. Then divide the children into small groups and give each group a card with one vocabulary word on it. Each group discusses how to act out the vocabulary word. Then groups take turns acting out the words while the others guess the word.

ELL Ask English learners to make word cards for the vocabulary words. On one side, ask the children to write the word; on the other side, ask the children to draw a picture to show the meaning of the word. If it would aid in their understanding, encourage the children to write the word in their home language on the side with the picture.

TARGET SKILL AND STRATEGY

CAUSE AND EFFECT Explain to children that an *effect* is what happened, and the *cause* is why it happened. Ask children to identify the cause and effect in sentences, for example, "The Chrysler company put hub cap shapes on its building because it was a car company."

PREDICT/CONFIRM PREDICTIONS Point out to children that as they read, they should think about what information might come next. Remind them that readers often use what they already know to make predictions. Ask: What do you know about buildings that helped you predict what you would read about?

ADDITIONAL SKILL INSTRUCTION

DRAW CONCLUSIONS Explain to children that when they read a book and look at the pictures, they can use what they have read and what they know from real life to figure out more. Tell them that this is called *drawing a conclusion*. Give the children an example from their lives. Then ask them what kind of conclusions they can make after reading this book.

Name _____

Cause and Effect

Circle the best answer for each question below.

I. Why does a building in New York City have the shapes of cars on it?

It was built from many car parts.

A company that makes cars built it.

It was built to hold a lot of cars.

---

2. Why are gargoyles on some buildings?

Gargoyles make a building strong.

Gargoyles are scary.

Gargoyles help the rain run off the roof.

---

3. Why did someone put a griffin on a museum?

Someone wanted people to think the museum was smart and strong.

Someone wanted people be afraid of the museum.

Someone wanted people to think that the museum was a zoo.

---

4. Why did the school put a face of a boy on one side of the doorway and a girl on the other side?

The school wanted the girls to go home.

The school wanted to scare both boys and girls.

The school wanted to welcome all children.

---

5. Why are there eagles on government buildings?

The eagle is our national bird.

Eagles are found in many parks.

People have eagles as pets.

Name _____

Vocabulary

Circle the word under each sentence that best completes the sentence.

1. I _____ in a house with lots of trim.
   discover   dwell

2. Most _____ buildings have eagles on them.
   government   resident

3. If you look at special buildings, you will _____
   welcome   discover
   many shapes.

4. _____ help the rain run off the roof.
   Griffins   Gargoyles

5. Every morning the teachers _____ the children
   resident   welcome
   to class.

6. Now, when you see a _____, you will know it is
   griffin   gargoyle
   strong and smart.

7. Whether you are a _____ of a town or a city,
   resident   dwell
   there are special buildings to see.

Grasshopper and Ant

SUMMARY In this retelling of the Aesop fable, a playful grasshopper learns that he should have worked hard like his neighbor the ant to make sure he had food for the winter. The story supports the lesson concept that some problems need clever solutions.

LESSON VOCABULARY

clever   intend
predicament

INTRODUCE THE BOOK

INTRODUCE THE TITLE AND AUTHOR Discuss with children the title and author of *Grasshopper and Ant*. Tell children that this story is a fable. Lead a short discussion of the genre, and ask children to share any fables they know.

BUILD BACKGROUND Discuss with children what they know about insects and the food they eat. Ask: Do most plants grow in the winter? What problems would an animal that eats plants have during the winter?

PREVIEW Have children preview by looking at the pictures in the book. Ask: What are the ant and the grasshopper doing during most of the story? Have children read the heading on page 16. Ask: Why do you think the author included this page in the book?

READ THE BOOK

SET PURPOSE Have children set a purpose for reading *Grasshopper and Ant*. Ask children to think about the plot elements they noticed in their preview. Ask: What do you want to find out by reading this story?

STRATEGY SUPPORT: MONITOR AND CLARIFY
Remind children to *monitor*, or think about, what they are reading and stop and *clarify* anytime they hit a roadblock. Suggest that they ask themselves questions as they read and then keep on reading to find the answers. This will help them clarify what they are reading.

COMPREHENSION QUESTIONS

PAGES 3–6 How would you describe the ant and the grasshopper? *(Possible response: The ant works hard, and the grasshopper likes to play.)*

PAGE 8 Where did the grasshopper stay when it rained? *(under a big, leafy plant)*

PAGE 9 What happened after summer turned to fall? *(The ant worked harder, and the grasshopper sang and danced.)*

PAGE 13 What happened with the grasshopper? Why did it happen? *(He was cold and hungry and did not have any food. It happened because he played instead of worked.)*

PAGE 15 Suppose the characters in this story were two children, and the story happened in school. How would you change the plot? *(Possible response: I would have one child listen to the teacher and the other child fool around.)*

REVISIT THE BOOK

THINK AND SHARE

1. Characters: Grasshopper and Ant; Setting: Long ago, at the edge of a field; Plot: Ant works hard to get ready for the winter, and Grasshopper plays and dances all day. When winter comes, Ant is comfortable in his home and Grasshopper is cold outside. Grasshopper asks Ant if he could have some food, but Ant says no.

2. Possible response: I can stop and ask myself questions. I can read on in the story to see if I can find the answer. This will help me clarify what I'm reading.

3. Possible responses: lived/live, liked/like, dancing/dance, singing/sing, carried/carry, watched/watch, worked/work

4. Possible response: Yes, because the ant would go hungry too.

EXTEND UNDERSTANDING Have children look at page 16. Explain that ants really do work in real life, and grasshoppers hop around. That is why the author chose them to represent hard work and playfulness.

RESPONSE OPTIONS

WORD WORK Write the lesson vocabulary on the chalkboard. Give children the following paragraph on paper: *I thought I was intend when I bought three ice cream cones for the price of two. But I didn't predicament for them to melt before I ate them. What a clever!* Say: This story uses all the vocabulary words, but it doesn't make sense. That's because the vocabulary words are in the wrong places. Find the vocabulary words, and put them where they belong.

ELL Invite pairs of children to perform a skit based on *Grasshopper and Ant*. Encourage children to use their own words and gestures to portray the two characters in the story. Suggest that they say the moral of the story in unison at the end of their skit.

SCIENCE CONNECTION

Display information about how different animals, such as grasshoppers, bears, deer, and squirrels survive the winter. Have children work together to make a wall display to classify animals by how they deal with food in the winter: following food, storing food, and hibernating.

Skill Work

TEACH/REVIEW VOCABULARY

Write the words *clever, cozy, intend, predicament,* and *relax* on the chalkboard. Then, write: *I didn't mean to talk.* Ask: Which word could you use to replace *mean*? Repeat by replacing case and smart in these sentences: It's a sad case when you don't have money. The smart girl figured out a way to help.

TARGET SKILL AND STRATEGY

CHARACTER, SETTING, AND PLOT Remind children that a *character* is the person or animal that the story is about. Remind them also that *setting* is the "where and when" of a story, and that the *plot* describes what happens in the story. Have children pay attention to these three things as they read the story.

MONITOR AND CLARIFY Remind children that what they read should make sense. When they find an unfamiliar word, they can find out what it means by looking in a dictionary or glossary.

ADDITIONAL SKILL INSTRUCTION

CAUSE AND EFFECT Demonstrate *cause and effect* by holding some pencils in your fist and then opening your hand. Ask: What happened to the pencils? (*They fell.*) Why did this happen? (*You opened your hand.*) Ask children to ask themselves what happened and why it happened as they read the story. Explain that sometimes what happened and why it happened can be far apart in a story. Have children read pages 4–6. Ask: What happened with the ant? (*He worked hard.*) Why did it happen? (*Winter was coming.*)

Name _____

Character, Setting, and Plot

Read part of *Grasshopper and Ant* below. Think about what it tells you about the **characters**, **setting**, and **plot** of the story. Then circle the correct answers to the questions.

> As summer turned to fall, the air got cooler.
>
> "Winter will be here before I know it!" thought the ant. So he worked even harder than he did before.
>
> The grasshopper kept on singing and dancing. "You are so boring!" he said to the ant. "Won't you come and dance with me?"

1. How many characters are in this part of the story?

   1   2   3

2. What season does this part of the story take place in?

   fall   summer   winter

3. Which word describes the ant?

   lazy   sleepy   hardworking

4. Think about the whole story. When in the story did this part happen?

   beginning   middle   end

110

Vocabulary

Write the word from the box that best completes each sentence.
You may use a word more than once.

> **Words to Know**
>
> clever   intend   predicament

1. At the end of the story, the grasshopper was in the snow without food.

   _____

   He was in a bad _____.

2. The ant thought about the winter.

   _____

   He did not _____ to be without food.

3. The ant was not in a _____ because he had prepared for the winter.

4. The ant organized his food.

   _____

   That showed that he was _____.

Ways to Be a Good Citizen

SUMMARY This informational reader gives the children a view of activities they can do at each step of their growth to age 18.

LESSON VOCABULARY

aquarium	citizen
community	freedom
miserable	selfish
teenager	tutor

INTRODUCE THE BOOK

INTRODUCE THE TITLE AND AUTHOR Discuss with children the title and the author of *Ways to Be a Good Citizen*. Based on the title and cover, ask what they think this book may be about.

BUILD BACKGROUND As you continue the discussion about the book, draw attention to the word *citizen*. Ask what they think being a good citizen means. Do they know anyone who looks like they are good citizens? If so, how do they show it?

PREVIEW/TAKE A PICTURE WALK Ask the children to leaf through the book, looking at the photos, illustrations, and captions and stopping at the ones that particularly interest them. Ask them to note the pages of interest because, when they read the book, they may want to learn more about the suggested activities that kids of that age are able to do.

READ THE BOOK

SET PURPOSE Return to your introduction to this book, reminding children that the discussion should help them to set their own purpose for reading this book. Their natural interest in being helpers will help to spur this purpose.

STRATEGY SUPPORT: BACKGROUND KNOWLEDGE Remind children that they can use what they already know as they read. Encourage children to use their background knowledge on page 4. Ask: Do you know any three-year-olds? How do they act? Do they like to share?

COMPREHENSION QUESTIONS

PAGE 3 What does *citizen* mean? *(a member of a place)*

PAGES 3–15 In what order did the author describe the activities for making a better world? *(He placed them by ages.)*

PAGE 6 At age 8, what kinds of activities can kids do? *(Possible responses: join clubs, clean parks)*

PAGE 10 What is a tutor and why does it help? *(a kind of teacher; helps kids to learn better individually)*

PAGE 11 In what special ways can teenagers help? *(go shopping for older people, serve food to the hungry, etc.)*

PAGE 12 Why is it so important to vote? *(It's the most special activity you can do as a citizen.)*

REVISIT THE BOOK

THINK AND SHARE

1. Possible response: they are selfless; they are kind; they like to help others
2. Responses will vary.
3. Sentences will vary.
4. Voters choose leaders and help decide what laws the community should follow.

EXTEND UNDERSTANDING As the children look at the ways that kids learn to help others as they grow up, suggest that they make their own "path to being a good citizen." Suggest that they draw themselves walking along a path, helping people in different ways as they get to be 9, 12, and 18 years old. Have them draw as much detail as they can imagine themselves doing at those ages.

RESPONSE OPTIONS

WORD WORK Ask the children to choose two or three words from the glossary that they like and use them as prompts for telling a story to a partner. For example, they could tell a story about a *selfish* and *miserable* superhero who wants to escape and get back the *freedom* to be his kind superhero self again.

SOCIAL STUDIES CONNECTION

Time For
SOCIAL
STUDIES

As the children complete the Good Citizen Project, ask them how they might share their project with the rest of the school. Talk about the effects of having the larger community help to make this project reach even more people. For example, they might start with making posters from their own project.

Skill Work

TEACH/REVIEW VOCABULARY

Write the three vocabulary words on the board and draw the children's attention to them before they read the book. Invite children to create an illustrated list of activities that promote freedom and keep people from being selfish and miserable.

ELL Ask for volunteers to make up a short skit telling about a situation where some people had their freedom taken from them and how brave citizens helped to correct it.

TARGET SKILL AND STRATEGY

DRAW CONCLUSIONS Remind children that when they read a book and look at the pictures, they can use what they have read and what they know from real life to figure out more. Ask: What conclusion can you draw about the types of litter there is from the pictures on page 7? *(Possible response: Cans and tires are types of litter.)*

BACKGROUND KNOWLEDGE Tell children that *background knowledge* is what they already know from their own experiences, books they have read, of things other people have told them. As children read, encourage them to use their background knowledge whenever possible.

ADDITIONAL SKILL INSTRUCTION

COMPARE AND CONTRAST Use this reader to help children to recognize similarities and differences. You can show likenesses in how children at different ages want to help others, or be good citizens. You can show differences by drawing attention to the different activities kids can do at different ages. Ask children for their own activities ideas. From this discussion, point out ways to see likenesses and differences related to this topic.

Name _____

Draw Conclusions

Use *Ways to Be a Good Citizen* to draw two conclusions about how being a good citizen is good for our world.

1.

_____
_____
_____
_____
_____
_____
_____
_____
_____

2.

_____
_____
_____
_____
_____
_____
_____
_____

Name _____

Vocabulary

Read the sentences below and choose the best word from the box to complete each one. **Write** the word on the line.

Words to Know			
aquarium	citizen	community	freedom
miserable	selfish	teenager	tutor

1. Nobody likes to be with a _____ person.

2. You like to take care of fish in the _____ .

3. When you feel _____, help others.

4. Some kids join clubs in the _____ .

5. Have you ever had a _____ help you?

6. Teenagers have _____ to help away from home.

7. When you are a _____, where will you help?

8. What can a _____ do at age 18?

Great Scientists: Detectives at Work

◉ **COMPARE AND CONTRAST**
◉ **MONITOR AND CLARIFY**

SUMMARY This nonfiction book is about how a scientist often works like a detective, searching for answers to mysteries. It gives examples of various types of scientists and some ways that they solve mysteries.

LESSON VOCABULARY

explanation	fossil
investigators	record
riddle	stump
wonder	

INTRODUCE THE BOOK

INTRODUCE THE TITLE AND AUTHOR Discuss with children the title and the author of *Great Scientists: Detectives at Work*. Based on the title, ask children what kind of information they think this book will provide. Ask: Who is the person in the cover illustration?

BUILD BACKGROUND Discuss what children know about detectives. Ask if they know anyone who works for the police department. Then discuss what children know about scientists. Ask: What kinds of things do scientists do?

PREVIEW/TAKE A PICTURE WALK Have children flip through the book, looking at the photos and reading the captions. Point out the variety of objects in the photos on pages 10–11. Ask: What do you think scientists try to do? (*solve problems*) Then point out the tools on pages 12–13. Ask: What are these tools? Why do scientists use them?

ELL Have children look at the photos and read the captions on pages 12–13. Then point to each object in the photos and ask students to say the English word for it and the word for it in their home language. Have them say in English what they know about each object.

READ THE BOOK

SET PURPOSE Have children set a purpose for their reading. As they look at the photos in the book, ask: What questions do you have about the photos? What do you want to learn from this book?

STRATEGY SUPPORT: MONITOR AND CLARIFY Remind children that *monitoring* one's comprehension is to be aware of whether or not you understand the text and that one must clarify misunderstandings of the text. Encourage children to stop reading when they find that they no longer understand the text. Then, have them write down the things that they do know about the text to see if they can clarify their understanding. If this doesn't help, they should go back and reread to find the answers to their questions. Have children write down the answers to their own questions.

COMPREHENSION QUESTIONS

PAGE 3 How do detectives solve mysteries? (*They search for an explanation, they look for clues, and they ask a lot of questions and pay close attention to the answers.*)

PAGE 6 How are the jobs of scientists and detectives alike? (*Possible response: They have big questions, they look for clues to help find the answer, and they study the clues to find facts.*)

PAGE 6 What is a fact? (*information that is known to be true*)

PAGE 9 How can you tell how old a tree is? (*by counting its rings*)

PAGES 12–13 What kinds of tools do scientists and detectives use? (*notebooks, computers, tape recorders, cameras*)

REVISIT THE BOOK

THINK AND SHARE

1. Possible responses: Alike: They both ask questions, try to find answers, use five senses. Different: scientists work in labs, detectives solve crimes
2. Possible responses: look at the pictures, reread, read on
3. Drawings will vary, but should reflect an understanding of the vocabulary.
4. Responses will vary.

EXTEND UNDERSTANDING Have children perform the activity on pages 14 and 15. Then, discuss the five senses. Ask: How do your senses keep you out of danger? (*Possible responses: Sight helps me look both ways before I cross the street. Hearing helps me hear warnings shouted by people. Smell can help me detect a fire.*) Ask: How else do your senses inform you about your surroundings? (*Possible responses: Smell alerts me to when my parents fix dinner or when my mom bakes cookies.*)

RESPONSE OPTIONS

WRITING Have children write down a "big question" that they have. Then, have them write down ways that they would go about finding answers. Model a question and detecting process: "I want to know how plants grow, so I am going to look in a book about plants to find out."

WORD WORK Write the vocabulary words on the chalkboard. Then read sentences to children, leaving the vocabulary word blank. Have children write down the correct word to fill in the blank.

SCIENCE CONNECTION

TIME FOR
Science

Have children read about dinosaur discoveries. When they learn the name of the scientist (or archaeologist) who discovered the important fossils, have them draw the scientist with his or her discovery.

Skill Work

TEACH/REVIEW VOCABULARY

Review vocabulary words with children. Have them write down the words and the definitions. Model how to use the words in a sentence. Then have students use each word in a sentence.

TARGET SKILL AND STRATEGY

COMPARE AND CONTRAST Tell children: *Compare* means telling how things are the same. *Contrast* means telling how things are different. Ask: How are scientists and detectives alike? How are they different?

MONITOR AND CLARIFY Remind students that good readers know to *monitor* their understanding as they read to make sure that the story makes sense to them. Model the awareness of not understanding confusing points in the text: "I don't understand what this means." Tell children that good readers ask themselves questions about what they do not understand and *clarify* any problems they have in reading. Suggest that children can reread to figure out how things are alike or different in the book.

ADDITIONAL SKILL INSTRUCTION

MAIN IDEA AND DETAILS Tell children that a *main idea* is what an article is all about. The main idea gives the gist of a story. Guide students in identifying the main idea in *Great Scientists: Detectives at Work*. Explain that both scientists and detectives find answers to riddles, or questions that may seem not to have answers. Other information in the story provides *details* that support this main idea.

Name _____

Compare and Contrast

Read the sentences. Write **Scientist** on the line if the sentence is only about scientists. Write **Detective** if the sentence is only about detectives. Write **Both** if the sentence is about both scientists and detectives.

1. They must remember what they've learned and ask questions they need to ask.

_____

2. They solve crimes.

_____

3. They can make flavors for gum or candy.

_____

4. People hire them to find out where someone or something might be.

_____

5. They work hard to find the answers to their questions.

_____

Name _____

Vocabulary

Write the word or words that best fit each sentence.

Words to Know
explanation   fossil   investigators   record
riddle   stump   wonder

1. The scientist came up with an _____ for _____ why the dinosaur _____ was found in the desert.

2. The _____ asked a lot of questions to try to solve the crime.

3. I can count the rings on a tree _____ .

4. The investigator would _____ the information in his notebook.

5. I _____ how to solve the _____ .

Simple Machines in Compound Machines

SUMMARY This book describes the six different kinds of simple machines and several different compound machines that simple machines can combine to form, such as scissors and wheelbarrows.

LESSON VOCABULARY

compound machines	convenient
equipment	force
gadget	simple machines

INTRODUCE THE BOOK

INTRODUCE THE TITLE AND AUTHOR Discuss with children the title and author of *Simple Machines in Compound Machines*. Draw children's attention to the content triangle on the cover. Ask: What other books about science have you read? How do you think this book will relate to science?

BUILD BACKGROUND Remind children that we use both simple and compound machines every day. Ask: What do you think of when you hear the word *machine*? Discuss machines children may have used, such as scissors, bicycles, skateboards, merry-go-rounds, and seesaws. Encourage children to think about how machines simplify work by asking: How would you cut a piece of paper if you had no scissors? If the wheel had not been invented, how would we get from one place to another?

ELL Invite children to share home-language words related to simple and compound machines, such as the words for *push, pull, energy,* or *force*.

PREVIEW/TAKE A PICTURE WALK Have children read the title and spend a few minutes looking at the photos and labels. Discuss what these suggest about the selection's content. Look at the pictures on pages 8-9. Ask: What do these two scenes tell us? Why did the author put these scenes next to each other? What do all the pictures in the selection have in common?

READ THE BOOK

SET PURPOSE Guide children to set their own purposes for reading. Children's interest in machines (including moving toys) should guide this purpose. Suggest that children imagine times when they have used simple or complex machines to do something.

STRATEGY SUPPORT: SUMMARIZE As children read, extracting the main ideas for the purpose of summarizing will help them understand and retain what they read. Help young children learn to summarize by suggesting that they retell in their own words as much of the selection as they recall. As an aid, if necessary, draw up a list of the types of simple and compound machines mentioned in this selection.

COMPREHENSION QUESTIONS

PAGE 3 Write the main idea. *(Simple machines and compound machines make work easier.)*

PAGE 8 What are two important details about an inclined plane? *(Possible response: It's higher on one end, and it has a flat surface.)*

PAGE 9 How does a wedge work? *(It uses force to go between two things.)*

PAGE 13 Read the sentence containing the word *convenient*. Give another example of a convenient gadget. *(Possible responses: pencil sharpeners, stapler, or can opener)*

REVISIT THE BOOK

THINK AND SHARE

1. Simple machines: There are six kinds of simple machines. Each works in a different way. Compound machines: Compound machines are made out of two or more simple machines working together.
2. Possible response: There are two kinds of machines, simple and compound. Compound machines are made of simple machines.
3. Possible reponses should show how machines make things more convenient.
4. A simple machine does work with just one movement, while a compound machine combines two or more simple machines and involves more than one movement.

EXTEND UNDERSTANDING Go over the photos and pictures in the selection. Ask children to note what the pictures have in common. Guide children to use the pictures to understand the difference between simple and compound machines. Ask: What do these pictures tell you that you don't learn from the words?

RESPONSE OPTIONS

VIEWING Bring in or have children bring in examples from books, magazines, or the Internet of many different kinds of simple and compound machines. Include pictures of machines used in different historical eras, such as ramps used to build medieval fortresses or modern bridges or scaffolding. Also include mechanical or moving toys.

SCIENCE CONNECTION

Have children choose a favorite toy that incorporates a simple or compound machine, such as a skateboard or a yo-yo. Ask them to describe as accurately as they can in words or pictures how the machine works and how it helps the toy move.

Skill Work

TEACH/REVIEW VOCABULARY

Reinforce comprehension by passing out clues to each vocabulary word on index cards. Divide children into three groups, one for each vocabulary word. Ask each group to identify the correct vocabulary word and then use gestures, pictures, or synonyms to convey that word to the other groups.

TARGET SKILL AND STRATEGY

MAIN IDEA Tell children that a *main idea* is what an article is all about. The main idea gives the gist of a selection. Guide students in identifying the main idea of *Simple Machines in Compound Machines* by asking: What do you see on every page of this article? What do all the pictures have in common? What do the headings tell you? For first graders, a phrase or simple sentence such as *Simple machines make up complex machines* can adequately express the main idea.

SUMMARIZE Explain to children that a summary of an article is a brief statement that gives the main idea but leaves out unimportant details. Invite children to recall the important ideas of the article and restate them in their own words.

ADDITIONAL SKILL INSTRUCTION

CAUSE AND EFFECT Tell children that a cause is why something happens, and an effect is what happens. Give an example: "Using a wheelbarrow to move a heavy load is a cause; the effect is that it is easier to move the load." Focusing on simple machines, compound machines, or physical activities, invite children to think of other cause-and-effect relationships. Point out that sometimes one cause may have more than one effect.

Name _____

Main Idea

A **main idea** is the most important idea about a passage or group of sentences.

Directions Read the sentences below.

> A seesaw is a type of lever. The lever is a very simple machine. If you push down on one end, the other end goes up. A lever can be great for lifting things. You can also pull a lever up. When you do that, the other end goes down. That is a useful thing, too. Think of a wheelbarrow. Its handles are levers. When you lift them up, the wheelbarrow tilts down. Then you can roll the wheelbarrow.

I. What is the best title for this section? Circle it.

   a. How to Lift   **b.** Useful Things

   c. Levers   **d.** Wheelbarrows

Directions Read the sentences below.

> A compound machine is made up of two or more simple machines working together. Scissors, for example, are made of levers, wedges, and screws. Wheelbarrows are made of levers and wheels and axles. Shovels are made of wedges and levers.

2. What is the best title for this section? Circle it.

   a. Scissors   **b.** Simples Machines in Compound Machines

   c. Screws   **d.** Levers and Wedges

Name _____

Vocabulary

Read the sentences below. Fill in each blank with the correct word from the box.

Words to Know

compound machines   convenient
equipment   force
gadget   simple machine

1. A can opener is an example of a useful household

   _____

   _____ that is a compound machine.

2. Using machines is a _____ way to get work done quickly.

3. Many types of heavy _____ are made of compound machines.

4. It takes less _____ to push a box up a ramp than it does to lift it.

5. A wedge is a _____ _____.

6. Machines made of two or more simple machines are called

   _____ _____

   _____ _____.

Telephones Over the Years

◉ SEQUENCE
◉ TEXT STRUCTURE

SUMMARY This book tells the history of the telephone. It supports and extends the lesson concept that the invention of the telephone improved communication in our world.

LESSON VOCABULARY

automatic	determined
inventor	system
technology	

INTRODUCE THE BOOK

INTRODUCE THE TITLE AND AUTHOR Discuss with children the title and author of *Telephones Over the Years.* Say: Many scientific inventions have improved our world. How might this book have something to do with that?

BUILD BACKGROUND Ask children to share what they know about using a telephone. Lead a discussion of this question: Do you think telephones have changed from long ago?

PREVIEW/TAKE A PICTURE WALK Have children preview the pictures, captions, and labels in the book. Ask: What do you see in these pictures and photos? Why are there so many captions and labels? What kind of book is this?

READ THE BOOK

SET PURPOSE Have children set a purpose for reading *Telephones Over the Years.* Remind children of what they discussed when the title and author were introduced.

STRATEGY SUPPORT: TEXT STRUCTURE Tell children that as they read this book, they will see many dates. These dates will help them be able to put the events in sequence, or order. As children read, encourage them to use dates to keep track of how telephones have been changed over the year.

COMPREHENSION QUESTIONS

PAGE 5 How could a call from New York reach London in less than a minute? *(Electricity travels very quickly.)*

PAGE 9 Why did the telephone get smaller over time? *(Possible response: The technology used for making phones got better.)*

PAGES 10–11 When calls were made on early phones, what happened first, next, and last? *(First: Call the operator. Next: Operator puts call through switchboard. Last: The phone rings at the place you are trying to reach.)*

PAGE 12 How were push-button phones better than phones with dials? *(Pushing buttons is faster than dialing each number.)*

REVISIT THE BOOK

THINK AND SHARE

1. Answers and drawings will vary, but children should choose three telephones from the book and put them in the correct sequence.
2. Possible response: It helps me see how telephones have gotten smaller and better over time.
3. Possible response: The racer was *determined* to win. The *inventor* made a new machine. New *technology* makes smaller phones.
4. Answers will vary.

EXTEND UNDERSTANDING Guide children to use the glossary when they read a word that they don't understand.

RESPONSE OPTIONS

WRITING Have children describe the inventors Alexander Bell and Almon Strowger and their contributions to telephone development.

SCIENCE CONNECTION

Have children do guided research on the Internet to find out how a call travels from one cell phone to another. Ask them to draw a labeled diagram that illustrates the process.

TIME FOR
Science

Skill Work

TEACH/REVIEW VOCABULARY

Have children pair up and write a cloze sentence for one of the vocabulary words. Tell them to exchange sentences and fill in the correct word. Repeat the activity until all the words have been used at least once.

TARGET SKILL AND STRATEGY

SEQUENCE Say: As you read, think about what happens first, next, and last. After reading page 4, model: I read that several things happened after people wanted telephones. What happened first, next, and last? After children have read page 9, have them use a sequence chart to list how phones changed first, next, and last. Encourage children to use sequence charts to keep track of what happens.

TEXT STRUCTURE Remind children that the author uses dates to show how telephones have changed over time. Ask: What is the earliest date in this book? *(1876)* Why do you think this is the earliest this book goes back to? *(Possible response: This book is about telephones, and 1876 was when the telephone was first invented.)*

ELL Help children understand some of the technology terms in the book by pointing to the following in the photos and illustrations: dial, mouthpiece, operator, receiver, switchboard.

ADDITIONAL SKILL INSTRUCTION

DRAW CONCLUSIONS Model: On page 5, it says that phone wires were strung across the country, and then in 1927 phone calls could be made across the ocean. I know that the ocean is too deep for telephone poles. Based on what I read and what I know, I think the telephone lines must have been laid under water.

Name _____

Sequence

Put the events from *Telephones Over the Years* in the correct order by writing 1–5 on the lines.

_____ 1. Almon Strowger invented an automatic phone system.

_____ 2. People started using cordless phones.

_____ 3. The first telephone was built by the inventor Alexander Graham Bell.

_____ 4. The very first cell phone was made.

_____ 5. New Haven became the first city to have a telephone.

Name _____

Vocabulary

Write a word from the box that best completes each sentence about the book.

You may use a word more than once.

Words to Know
automatic   determined   inventor
system   technology

1. Almon Strowger was an _____.

2. New Haven, Connecticut, had the first telephone _____.

3. Inventors are _____ to make their ideas work.

4. Telephone systems use different kinds of _____.

5. Almon Strowger invented an _____ phone system.

Cody's Adventure

SUMMARY This realistic fiction book tells the story of Cody, who learns from his Aunt Janet how to paint rocks. Back home, Cody has an idea to make the new town library look much more inviting. He goes to a town meeting, gets permission, and then recruits others to help him decorate the library with a "rock garden."

LESSON VOCABULARY

accomplish   doubt

original   recognized

INTRODUCE THE BOOK

INTRODUCE THE TITLE AND AUTHOR Discuss with children the title and author of *Cody's Adventure*. Based on the title, ask children to tell what they think this book will be about. Have them look at the cover and guess where Cody spends some of his time.

BUILD BACKGROUND Ask children to tell what they know about fixing up a place so that it looks better. Ask: What kinds of things can people do to make a place look better? Discuss a place in the community that people may have worked together to make look better. Explain that Cody has an idea to make his town library look better.

PREVIEW/TAKE A PICTURE WALK Invite children to look through the illustrations in the book. Ask them to point out details they find interesting. Ask: What questions do you have as you look at the pictures in this book? Do you think these questions will be answered by the end of the story?

READ THE BOOK

SET PURPOSE Have children set a purpose for reading *Cody's Adventure*. Encourage their interest by explaining that Cody got an idea for making someplace in his community look a lot better. They may want to read to find out about that.

STRATEGY SUPPORT: INFERRING Explain to children that they can learn many things about the story or the characters without being told. Sometimes you can *infer* from the pictures in the book, and other times you can *infer* from the character's actions. Encourage children to infer as they read *Cody's Adventure*.

COMPREHENSION QUESTIONS

PAGE 3 What is Cody looking for with his Aunt Janet? *(rocks)*

PAGE 4 What do Cody and Aunt Janet do with the rocks they find? *(paint them)*

PAGE 5 What did Cody's mom suggest they do? *(go to the grand opening of the new library)*

PAGE 7 What is Cody's idea for making the new library look better? *(get kids to help him paint rocks like he does at Aunt Janet's)*

PAGE 11 What two good things happen to Cody? *(The town approves his idea; the paint store man donates paint and brushes.)*

REVISIT THE BOOK

THINK AND SHARE

1. Possible response: Kids can have big ideas.
2. Possible response: Excited; It made it easy to see why everyone else would like it.
3. Responses may be any five of the following words: *almost, over, opening, closer, also, know, go, told, phone, home, spoke,* and *Cody.*
4. Responses will vary but should take a child's idea and develop it with one or two details.

EXTEND UNDERSTANDING Invite children to look at the pictures on pages 6 and 14. Ask them to compare and contrast how the new library looks in the two illustrations. Ask: What do the pictures show you about Cody's idea to improve how the new library looks? Do you think he made the new library look better? Why do you think so? How did his Aunt Janet help with the painted rocks?

RESPONSE OPTIONS

WRITING Invite children to write a paragraph about the big idea of this story. What was it all about? For specific ideas, they can review the questions they generated during the picture walk.

SOCIAL STUDIES CONNECTION

Time For SOCIAL STUDIES

Children can help to bring about positive changes in their communities by working together with a esponsible adult or adults. Explain that it is usually necessary to ask for permission (as Cody's mother did) to make changes to public or private land, such as a vacant lot to be cleaned up and turned into a garden or a park. Ask children for an idea of a place they would like to see made better. Then talk with them about the steps they would take if they were to actually carry out their plan.

Skill Work

TEACH/REVIEW VOCABULARY

To reinforce the context for the meaning of *original,* have children turn to page 9. Read the page together. Ask children to explain how they used the context, or the other words in the paragraph, to help them understand the meaning of *original.* Continue in a similar fashion with the other vocabulary words.

TARGET SKILL AND STRATEGY

THEME Remind children that the theme is the "big idea," or lesson that the story teaches. Ask: What is *Cody's Adventure* mostly about? What do you think the theme is?

ELL Ask children if they remember a place people fixed up in their home country, and ask them to describe it. Ask: Did children play a role in making the place better?

INFERRING Remind children that when we *infer* something about the story we are reading, we are using pictures and the actions of characters to learn something we are not told. As they read *Cody's Adventure,* ask children inferring questions. For example, after reading page 9, ask: How do you think the people listening to the town hall meeting felt about Cody's idea? How can you tell? *(They liked it. The picture shows them smiling.)*

ADDITIONAL SKILL INSTRUCTION

SEQUENCE Remind children that sequence is what happens first, next, and last. Ask them to tell the sequence of events in this book. Say: First, Cody painted rocks with his Aunt Janet. Next, he went to the new library with his mother and the place looked very unfriendly. Last, Cody and his friends painted rocks, and the new library looked much better.

Name_____

Theme

Write the theme for *Cody's Adventure* in the box below. Then write three examples from the story that support this theme.

> **Theme**

1. _____
   -
   _____
   _____
   -
   _____

2. _____
   -
   _____
   _____
   -
   _____

3. _____
   -
   _____
   _____
   -
   _____

Name_____

Vocabulary

On the lines below, write about a time when you had an idea and carried it out. Use some of the vocabulary words from the box in your sentences.

Words to Know
accomplish   doubt   original   recognized

1-3. _____

_____

_____

_____

_____

4. Draw a picture to illustrate your story.

T-Chart

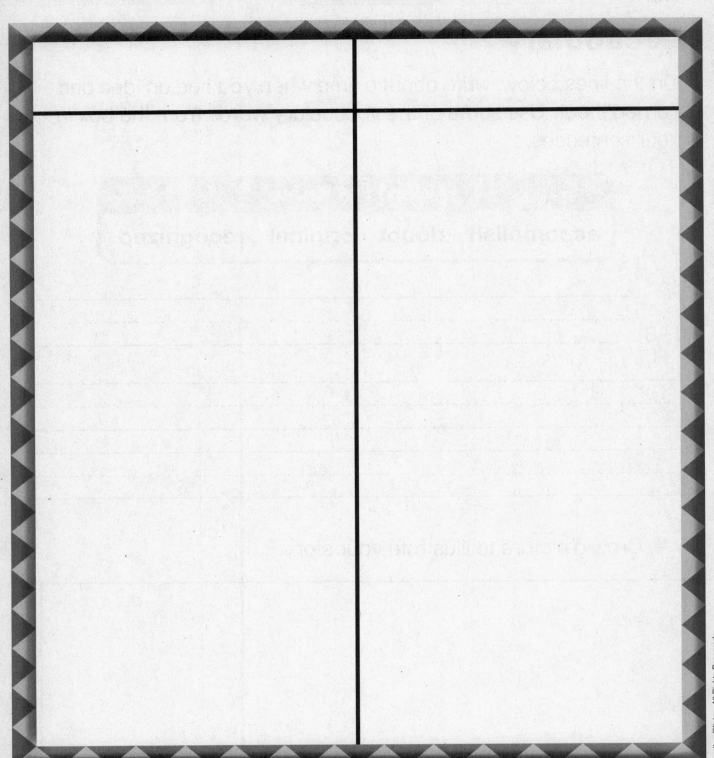

Suggestions You can use this chart to record information in two categories or for various sorting activities. Write the heading at the top of each column.

Three-Column Chart

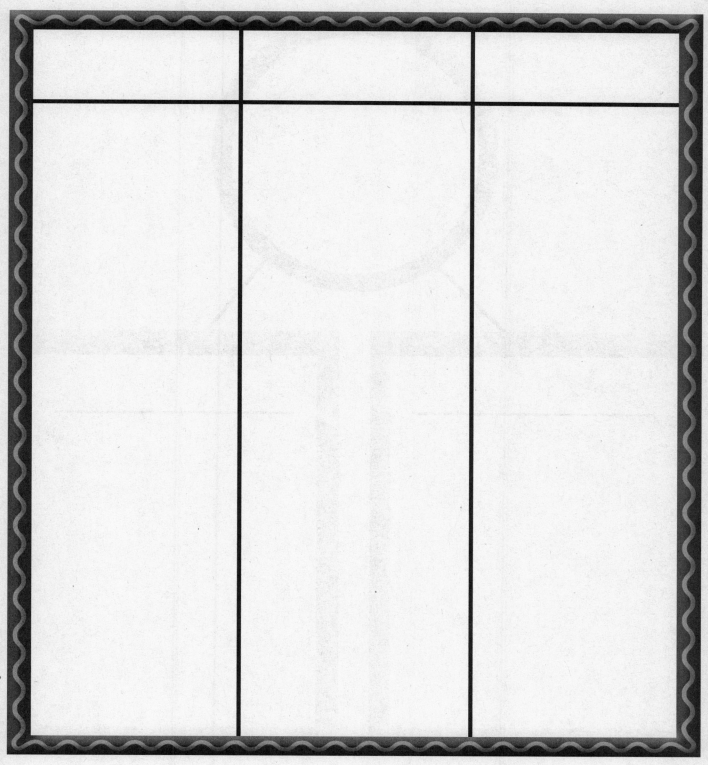

Suggestions You can use this chart to record information in three categories or for various sorting activities. Write the heading at the top of each column.

Classify

 Suggestions Children can use this chart to classify information. For example, pictures of animals could be placed in the circle and then sorted into land animals and water animals in the boxes below.

Pictograph

Title _____

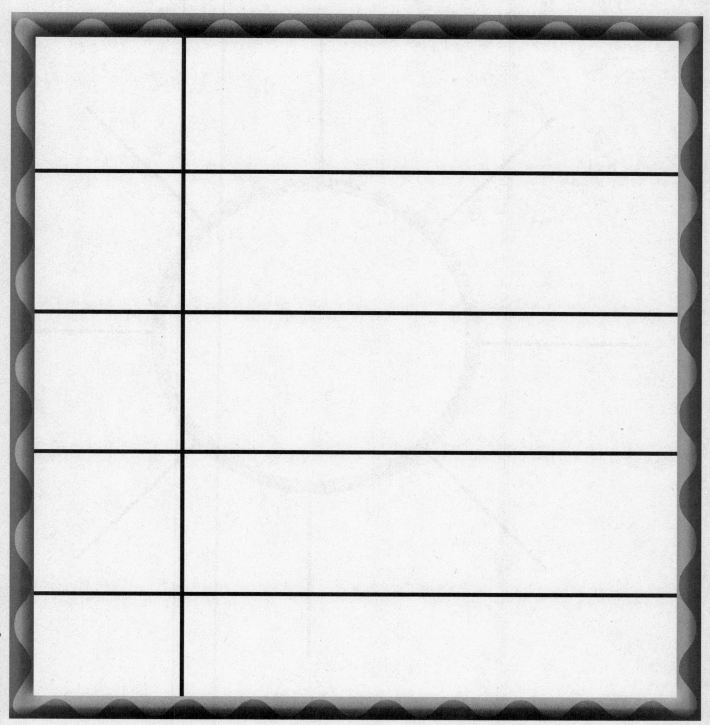

Suggestions Help children make a pictograph to record information. Children draw simple pictures on the chart or on self-stick notes to represent each item. Record the topic at the top of the chart. Some possible topics are: *What did we have for lunch? What pets do we have? What color shoes are we wearing?*

Web A

 Suggestions You can use this chart to activate children's prior knowledge about a topic. Write a major concept in the circle such as *Pets* or *Machines*. Children write or dictate words or ideas that relate to the concept. Write them so that the lines connect them to the circle.

Web B

 Suggestions You can use this chart to activate children's prior knowledge about a topic. Write a major concept in the middle circle, such as *Things at School.* In the smaller circles, children dictate words or ideas that relate to the concept. Additional ideas may be added on spokes coming from the smaller circles.

KWL Chart

K	W	L
What We Know	**What We Want to Know**	**What We Learned**

Suggestions Have children tell what they know or think they know about the topic. Record their responses in the column **What We Know.** Ask children what they would like to learn. List their questions in **What We Want to Know.** After children learn more about the topic, discuss what they learned. List children's responses in **What We Learned.**

Prediction

_____

_____

_____

_____

_____

_____

Suggestions You can use this chart to help children discuss predictions. Have children suggest what might happen next in a story or other situation. Children may draw a picture and dictate sentences to show the prediction.

Sequence

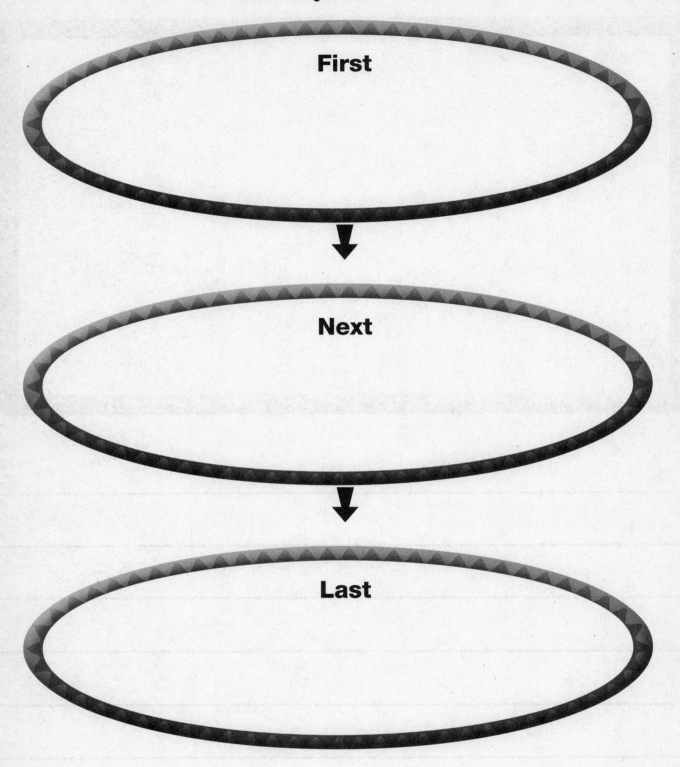

First

Next

Last

Suggestions Use this chart to help children place events in sequence. Children can draw pictures or dictate what happened first, next, and last.

Story Sequence A

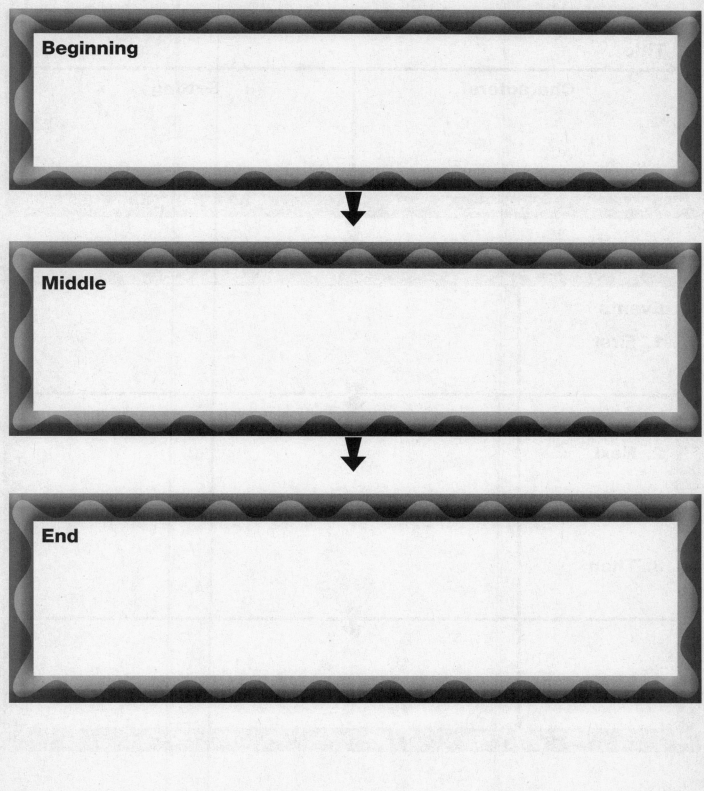

Beginning

Middle

End

Suggestions Use this chart to help children place events in a story in sequence. Children can draw pictures or dictate what happened in the beginning, middle, and end.

Story Sequence B

Title	
Characters	**Setting**

Events

1. First

2. Next

3. Then

4. Last

Suggestions After recording the title, characters, and setting of a story, children chart the sequence of events. This organizer helps children understand how one event leads to another.

Book Report

Title _____

Author _____

Illustrator _____

Setting _____

Characters _____

Our Favorite Parts _____

Suggestions You can use this chart to record information about a big book or trade book. Discuss where the story takes place, what happens in the book, and how children feel about the book. Invite children to draw pictures of their favorite parts of the book.

Story Comparison

Title A

Characters

Setting

Events

Title B

Characters

Setting

Events

Suggestions Use this chart to help children compare story elements and structures. This type of activity prepares children for working with Venn diagrams. Children may illustrate or dictate these comparisons.

Question the Author

Title _____

Author _____ Page _____

1. What does the author tell you?	
2. Why do you think the author tells you that?	
3. Does the author say it clearly?	
4. What would make it clearer?	
5. How would you say it instead?	

Suggestions Use this chart to help children understand the author's purpose and the author's craft. Students analyze what was said, how well it was said, and how it might be said differently.

Main Idea

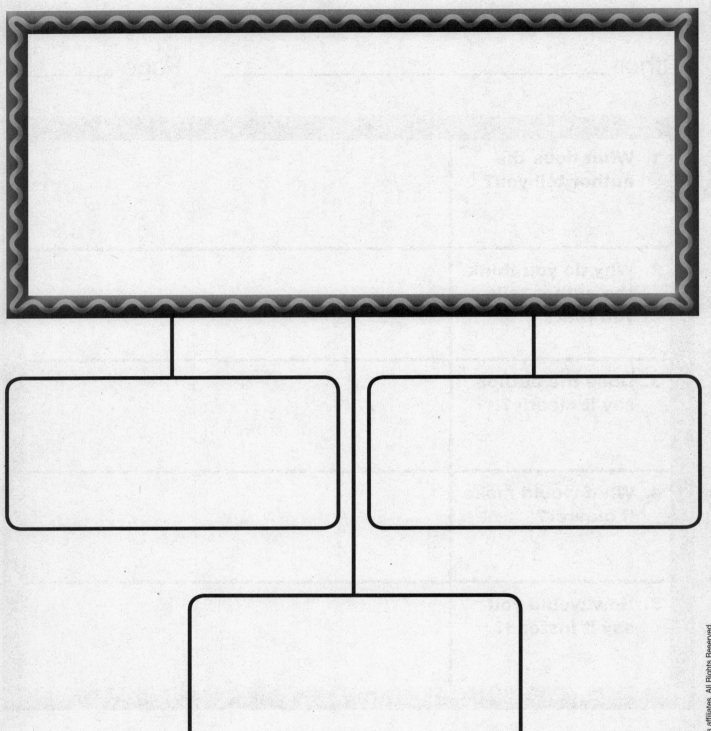

Suggestions Use this chart to help children understand the main idea of what they read. Ask: *What is the story all about?* Write children's responses in the top box. Have children draw or dictate in the smaller boxes other things they remember from the story.

Venn Diagram

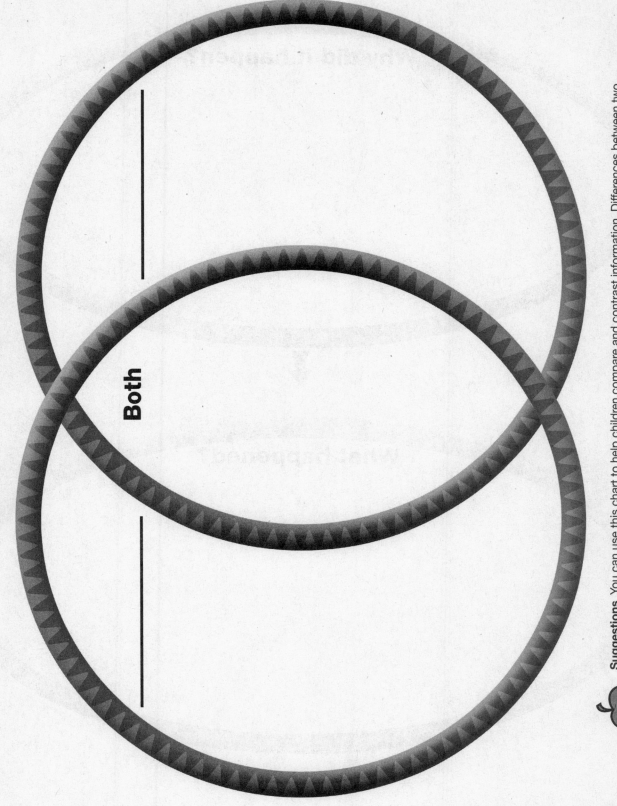

Both

Suggestions You can use this chart to help children compare and contrast information. Differences between two things being compared should be written in the non-intersecting portions. Similarities between two things being compared should be written in the intersection.

Cause and Effect

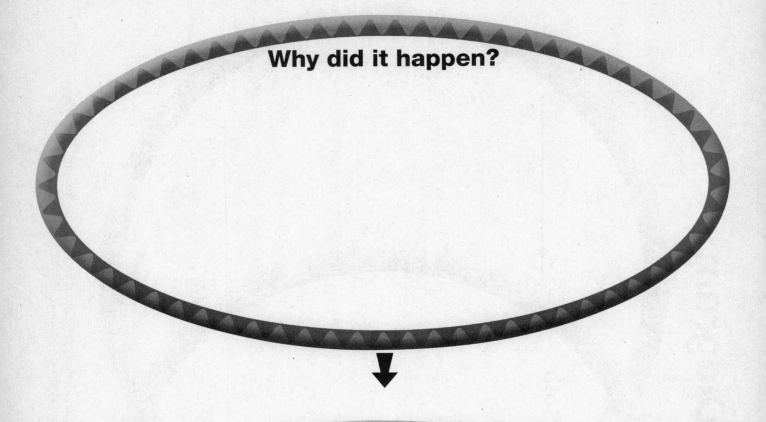

Why did it happen?

What happened?

Suggestions Use this chart to help children understand what happens (effect) and why it happens (cause). Children draw pictures in the appropriate ovals or dictate sentences to show an event. Help children think back and describe or draw what caused that event to happen.

Cycle Chart

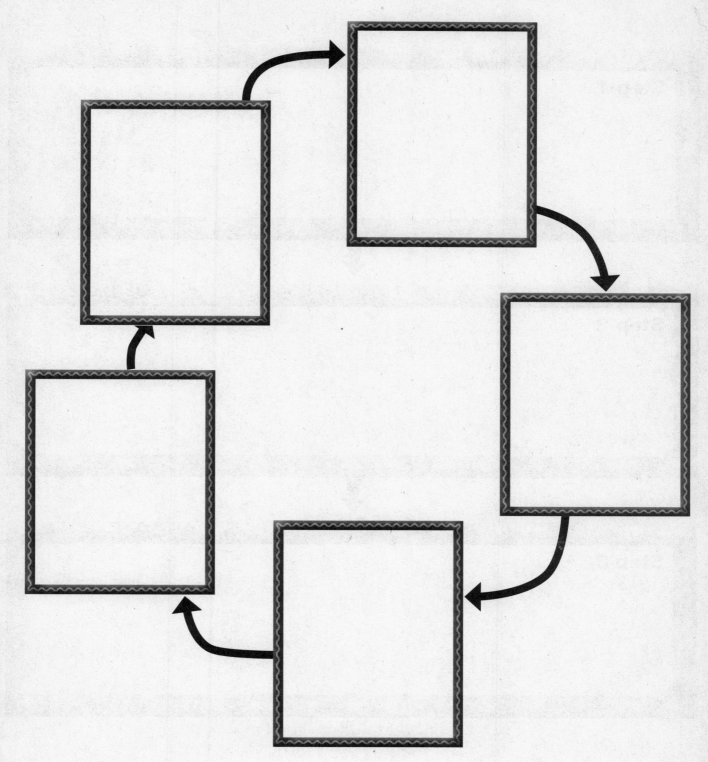

Suggestions Use this chart to help children understand how a series of events produces a series of results again and again. Discuss such questions as: *How does one event lead to another? What is the final outcome?* This chart works well for depicting life cycles.

Steps in a Process

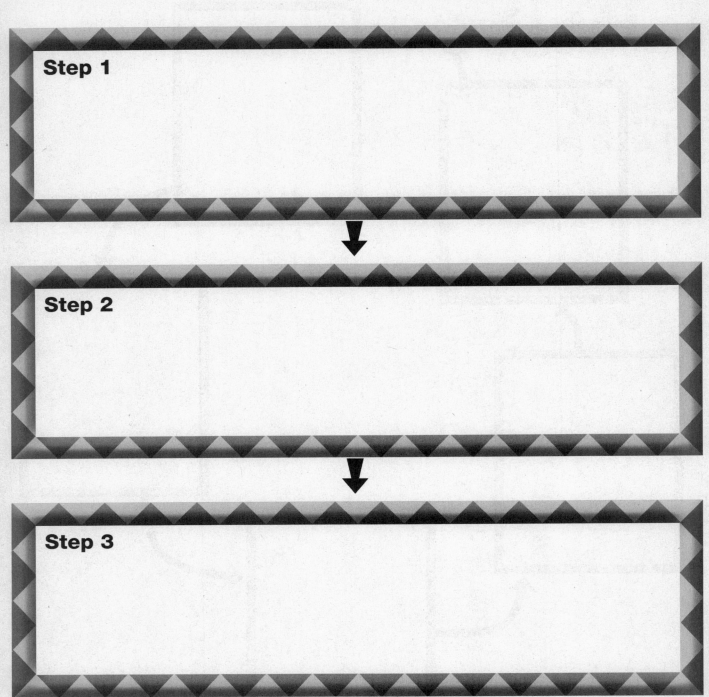

Step 1

Step 2

Step 3

Suggestions Use this chart to help children break down a process. This chart works well with a how-to activity that has a few simple steps. Students may draw pictures or dictate how to do something.

Writing Topics

Family	Friends	Pets

Hobbies	Favorite Activities

Special Places	Favorite Vacations

Happy Times	Times I Felt Proud

Suggestions Use this chart as a writing resource or interest inventory. Over time, children can generate numerous topics for future compositions.

Letter Format

Dear _____,

Suggestions Use this organizer to help children understand the format of a letter. The format can be used for writing to friends, family, or characters from a story.

Numbered List

Title _____

1. _____

2. _____

3. _____

4. _____

5. _____

Suggestions Use this chart to help children list characters, settings, problems, or items that can be found in different contexts or categories.

Answer Key

Leveled Reader Practice Pages

Carlos Picks a Pet p. 14
CHARACTER
Possible responses given.
1. Rabbits chew too many things.
2. Dogs need to go for walks.
3. Carlos likes cats the most.
4. Children's drawings should reflect that they understand the end of the story.

Carlos Picks a Pet p. 15 Vocabulary
1. responsibility
2. needs
3. shelter
Possible responses given.
4. I need food, water, and a place to live.
5. I help set the table at dinner.

That Cat Needs Help! p. 18
PLOT
Possible responses:
1. A cat is stuck in a tree.
2. Officer Kim
3. the fire department
4. The firefighter gets the cat down.

That Cat Needs Help! p. 19 Vocabulary
1. career
2. tools
3. service

Loni's Town p. 22
CHARACTER AND SETTING
Possible responses:
1. It has changed. She likes it.
2. happy to share her memories
3. glad to be with Loni
4. It has stores, houses, and people.
5. a little while ago

Loni's Town p. 23 Vocabulary
1. present
2. past
3. transportation
4. produce
5. Possible response: I live in a house in (name of the town).

Baby Animals in the Rain Forest p. 26
MAIN IDEA
1. baby monkeys
2. Possible response: Older monkeys watch younger ones. They give them rides on their back.

Baby Animals in the Rain Forest p. 27
Vocabulary
1. watch
2. born and living in nature
3. mother or father
4. Possible response: Every wild animal baby has a parent.

Cary and the Wildlife Shelter p. 30
MAIN IDEA
1. Some animals are losing their homes.
2. People are moving into the animals' natural habitats. People are building houses where the wild animals once lived.
3. Drawings will vary.

Cary and the Wildlife Shelter p. 31 Vocabulary
1. b
2. c
3. a
4. survive
5. habitat

Around the World p. 34
CAUSE AND EFFECT
1. Because there is little rain in the desert.
2. Because deserts are very dry.
3. Because their humps store food.
4. I went to school because it was Tuesday.

Around the World p. 35 Vocabulary
1. b
2. c
3. a
4. world
5. forest

Rules at School p. 38
SEQUENCE
1. 8
2. 3
3. 1
4. 6
5. 2
6. 9
7. 5
8. 10
9. 4
10. 7

Rules at School p. 39 Vocabulary
1. household
2. chores
3. rules
4. cooperation
5. Possible response: Teachers can count on students' cooperation.

School: Then and Now p. 42
CAUSE AND EFFECT
1. Underlined: The children went inside
   Circled: they heard the school bell
2. Underlined: the children got out their hornbooks
   Circled: the teacher said, "It's time to study the alphabet."
3. Underlined: they couldn't play after school.
   Circled: the children had to do chores.
4. Pictures should reflect an understanding of cause and effect.

School: Then and Now p. 43 Vocabulary
1. respect
2. group
3. share
4. Drawing should reflect an understanding of the meaning of these vocabulary words.

Mom the Mayor p. 46
AUTHOR'S PURPOSE
1. Possible response: It makes us think about being the son of a mayor.
2. Ramon is proud of his mom.

Mom the Mayor p. 47 Vocabulary
1. law
2. leader
3. citizen
4. community

The Dinosaur Detectives p. 50
SEQUENCE
Drawing and captions will vary. Possible captions given.
1. Dinosaur eating
2. Dinosaur dying
3. Fossil is formed
4. Someone finds a fossil

The Dinosaur Detectives p. 51 Vocabulary
1. enemy
2. protect
3. extinct
4. Answers will vary.

All About Food Chains p. 54
AUTHOR'S PURPOSE/POINT OF VIEW
1. living
2. energy
3. food chains

All About Food Chains p. 55 Vocabulary
Possible responses given.
1. a place in nature
2. the same as need
3. to grow successfully

Bees and Beekeepers p. 58
COMPARE AND CONTRAST
Wild Bees:
1. build their own homes
2. do not get special care
3. live in a hive
Beekeeper Bees:
4. homes built by beekeepers
5. get special care

Bees and Beekeepers p. 59 Vocabulary
1. Special means unique or different.
2. Industrious means busy.
3. Individual means one, single, or alone.

A New Library p. 62
SEQUENCE
1. Old library being torn down.
2. New foundation being dug.
3. Building frame being built.
4. Roof being put on.

A New Library p. 63 Vocabulary
1. population
2. public
3. makeshift
4. spindly
5. growth

Paul's Bed p. 66

COMPARE AND CONTRAST

1. They are alike because Paul is wearing a yellow shirt in both pictures.
2. They are alike because Paul is holding a boat in both pictures.
3. They are different because Paul is young in one picture and grown up in the other picture.
4. They are different because Paul is wearing overalls in one picture and jeans in the other picture.
5. Responses will vary but should tell how child feels about Paul's beds.

Paul's Bed p. 67 Vocabulary

1. event
2. attempt
3. time line
4. Sentence should reflect understanding of the words and the story.

Britton Finds a Kitten p. 70

FACT AND OPINION

1. a, d
2–3. Answers will vary, but students should include two facts from the story.

Britton Finds a Kitten p. 71 Vocabulary

mature, grown up; natural, normal; features, details
1–3. Students should show an understanding of the vocabulary word in their sentences.

All About the Weather p. 74

AUTHOR'S PURPOSE

1. grow
2. rain
3. weather

All About the Weather p. 75 Vocabulary

1. downpour
2. overcast
3. harsh
4–5. Sentences will vary but should use downpour and harsh correctly.

Learn About Butterflies p. 78

FACT AND OPINION

1. butterflies
2. chrysalis
3. crawl on flowers and taste
4. They camouflage the butterfly.
5. They help them fly away.

Learn About Butterflies p. 79 Vocabulary

1. insect
2. cycle
3. develop
4–5. Sentences will vary but should include facts from the story and the vocabulary words.

Monarchs Migrate South p. 82

DRAW CONCLUSIONS

Possible response: I think the cycle will begin all over again. The eggs will hatch, the caterpillars will grow, and then change into butterflies.

Monarchs Migrate South p. 83 Vocabulary

1. migrate, temperature
2. insect, nectar
3. hibernate, survive
4. Possible response: I am glad I don't have to hibernate or migrate every winter in order to survive.

Cascarones Are for Fun p. 86

DRAW CONCLUSIONS

1. Cascarones are made of eggshells.
2. Cascarones are fun and bring good luck.
3. The egg is first blown out.
4. It is easy to spread fun things.
5. Cascarones are made for celebrations.

Cascarones Are for Fun p. 87 Vocabulary

1. celebrate
2. China
3. perfume
4. Mexico
5. cherish
6. confetti
7. decorate
8. Italy
9. empress

Jamie's Jumble of Junk p. 90

1. Jamie saves a lot of junk in his room.
2. Jamie's school has a fair, and students need to make something original.
3. Jamie uses his imagination and recycled his junk to make a project for the fair.
4. Possible response: By using your imagination, you can recycle old things into new things.

Jamie's Jumble of Junk p. 91 Vocabulary
Possible responses given.
1. a Cub Scout shirt
2. a turkey
3. ribbon
4. a window
5. I think about what I will do when I am big.
6. A poem I wrote is original.
7. I rode on a carousel. I had a fabulous time.
8. I sighed when I got tired of waiting for my birthday to come.

America's Home p. 94
🔘 DETAILS AND FACTS
1. c
2. a
3. b
4. a
5. b

America's Home p. 95 Vocabulary
1. vote
2. symbol, nation
3. tourist
4. President, law
5. soldiers

Go West! p. 98
🔘 FACTS AND DETAILS
1. Her friend lives upstairs and her teacher was nice.
2. They left their dishes and the piano.
3. The train was noisy and the seats were hard.
4. Papa guided the mules and Sara held the reins.
5. Sara wanted to write in her notebook.

Go West! p. 99 Vocabulary
1. errand; a quick trip to do a job
2. familiar; something well known
3. favorite; best-liked
4. impression; an idea or feeling
5. memory; something you remember
6. stampede; a rush of wild animals
Responses will vary, but should reflect correct use of the vocabulary words in context.

Double Trouble Twins p. 102
🔘 THEME
Possible response: The theme of the story is that you should take the time to read things through before you do them.

Double Trouble Twins p. 103 Vocabulary
1. relatives
2. jealous
3. sibling
4. relatives
5. Illustrations will vary.

What Makes Buildings Special? p. 106
🔘 CAUSE AND EFFECT
1. A company that makes cars built it.
2. Gargoyles help rain run off the roof.
3. Someone wanted people to think the museum was smart and strong.
4. The school wanted to welcome all children.
5. The eagle is our national bird.

What Makes Buildings Special?
p. 107 Vocabulary
1. dwell
2. government
3. discover
4. Gargoyles
5. welcome
6. griffin
7. resident

Grasshopper and Ant p. 110
🔘 CHARACTER, SETTING, AND PLOT
1. 2
2. fall
3. hardworking
4. middle

Grasshopper and Ant p. 111 Vocabulary
1. predicament
2. intend
3. predicament
4. clever

Ways to Be a Good Citizen p. 114
🔘 DRAW CONCLUSIONS
1–2. Sentences will vary, but students should show an understanding of how being a good citizen is good for the world.

Ways to Be a Good Citizen p. 115 Vocabulary

1. selfish
2. aquarium
3. miserable
4. community
5. tutor
6. freedom
7. teenager
8. citizen

Great Scientists: Detectives at Work p. 118

COMPARE AND CONTRAST

1. Both
2. Detective
3. Scientist
4. Detective
5. Both

Great Scientists: Detectives at Work

p. 119 Vocabulary

1. explanation, fossil
2. investigators
3. stump
4. record
5. wonder, riddle

Simple Machines in Compound Machines

p. 122

MAIN IDEA

1. c
2. b

Simple Machines in Compound Machines

p. 123 Vocabulary

1. gadget
2. convenient
3. equipment
4. force
5. simple machine
6. compound machines

Telephones Over the Years p. 126

SEQUENCE

1. 3
2. 5
3. 1
4. 4
5. 2

Telephones Over the Years p. 127 Vocabulary

1. inventor
2. system
3. determined
4. technology
5. automatic

Cody's Adventure p. 130

THEME

Possible responses: Theme: Even little kids can have big ideas

1. Cody has the idea of painting rocks for the library.
2. Everybody likes Cody's idea.
3. The library makes a sign for Cody to thank him.

Cody's Adventure p. 131 Vocabulary

1–3. Responses will vary but should correctly use some of the four vocabulary words. Possible sentences: I want to accomplish a new look for my room. It was my original idea to hang posters of my favorite sport. My mom recognized my idea when she told my grandmother about it.
4. Pictures will vary but should reflect the idea(s) of what the child has written.